FACE TO FACE

FACE TO FACE

*A narrative essay
in the theology of suffering*

FRANCES YOUNG

T&T CLARK
EDINBURGH

T&T CLARK
59 GEORGE STREET
EDINBURGH EH2 2LQ
SCOTLAND

First published 1990

ISBN 0 567 29177 4

British Library Cataloguing in Publication Data
Young, Frances
Face to face.
1. Families with handicapped children
I. Title
362.4088054

Typeset by Trinity Typesetting, Edinburgh
Printed and bound in Great Britain by Billing & Sons Ltd, Worcester

CONTENTS

ACKNOWLEDGEMENTS

Chinua Achebe, *Anthills of the Savannah*, William Heine-
mann 1987, Pan books Ltd. 1988, is quoted by permission of David Holt Associates, authors' agents.

The Gospel of Anger © Alastair Campbell 1986, is reproduced
by permission of SPCK, London.

Eric Milner-White: *My God my Glory* © The Friends of York
Minster 1954, 1967, is reproduced by permission of
SPCK, London.

William Horwood, *Skallagrigg* is not directly quoted, but the
author would like to acknowledge her debt to the inspiration of that novel, published by Penguin Books,
1988.

PREFACE

This book owes much to many people, especially Iain Torrance who pushed me into doing something about developing the original, and Geoffrey Green of T & T Clark who encouraged it further. They were building on the prodding of correspondence and friends who wanted an up-date, or regretted the book's unavailability. It is to them that this enlarged version is offered. But mention must also be made of those who first provoked my telling the story, Valerie Edden and John Stacey of Epworth Press, and all those whose contribution was recognised in the original Preface, not least the stream of 'Arthur-sitters' and professionals who go on supporting us.

The story goes on even as the book goes through the publishing process, and some of the up-date is already history. Already the 'standing-box' has been retired, and we have just had to revert to carrying him downstairs. His physical deterioration is one of a number of factors which have turned his father into the principal carer. After early retirement, Bob is now Treasurer of Birmingham Mencap, and represents the Society on many local committees concerned with provision of services: Arthur has provided his father with a 'second (voluntary) career'.

Contact with disability groups has alerted me to an increasingly widespread uneasiness with the term 'handicap', and many now prefer to speak of those with 'learning difficulties'. I find this a bit incongruous when dealing with someone as profoundly handicapped as Arthur, though I appreciate the point when those less affected are trying to gain employment and social acceptance. I hope that readers will be prepared to meet me where I am, and ponder the comments on the language problem in chapter 8.

Direct quotations from scripture are from the Revised Standard Version. Other acknowledgements are indicated on p. viii and in notes or references in the text. Much of the text bears the marks of an original oral form, and the collection of a number of discrete lectures and talks in one place has occasioned the repetition of some examples. I hope the reader will bear with these features patiently.

March 1990   Frances M. Young

PART A
The Story

INTRODUCTION

'The sounding of the battle drum is important: the fierce waging of the war itself is important; and the telling of the story afterwards — each is important in its own way. . . . But if you ask me which of them takes the eagle-feather I will say boldly: the story. . . .

'Why? Because it is only the story that can continue beyond the war and the warrior. It is the story that outlives the sound of war-drums and the exploits of brave fighters. It is the story, not the others, that saves our progeny from blundering like beggars into the spikes of the cactus fence. The story is our escort; without it, we are blind. Does the blind man own his escort? No, neither do we the story; rather it is the story that owns us and directs us. It is the thing that makes us different from cattle; it is the mark on the face that sets one people apart from their neighbours. . . .

'So the arrogant fool who sits astride the story as though it were a bowl of foo-foo set before him by his wife understands little about the world. The story will roll him into a ball, dip him in the soup and swallow him first. I tell you he is like the puppy who swings himself around and farts into a blazing fire with the aim to put it out. Can he? No, the story is everlasting. . . . Like fire, when it is not blazing it is smouldering under its own ashes or sleeping and resting inside its flint-house.'

(Chinua Achebe, *Anthills of the Savannah*, 1987)

An African novel alerts us to the importance of the story in human consciousness. For it is indeed memory, both individual and corporate, that enables the development of identity, culture, understanding and the possibility of purposive action. It is the differentiation and selection of

1

significant features of experience, and their formation into narrative that enables us to make sense of things. Story-making is a step on the road to abstract analysis, and story-telling the most effective way of communicating collective experience and values. Stories are revealing.

The Judaeo-Christian tradition instinctively exploits this, though theological thinkers have often behaved as if they could emulate Achebe's puppy, speaking of God and human beings philosophically rather than narratively. An examination of the creeds, however, soon alerts us to their essentially narrative character, and the Bible is what Achebe's old African would call 'the story of the land', the collective memory, largely narrative, that gives members of God's people their identity and 'escort'.

The biblical story is 'journey-shaped', and encouraged the development of the notion of spiritual journey. Understanding becomes a pilgrimage, a process, rather than a comprehensive attainment. Christian theology, for all its indebtedness to Platonic ideas of Being, eternity, complete-ness and perfection, cannot eschew the reality of Becoming, of human incompleteness and progress through discipline and experience, response and relationship. So it is that 'testimony' belongs at the heart of Christianity, and the most effective theology is 'incarnated' in story.

So I make no apology for prefacing a collection of theological essays by the narrative experience which stimulated them, and including here in the introduction the 'testimony' which formed the Prelude to the original account of the story written in 1984 and published under the title *Face to Face* (Epworth 1985). The chapters which follow largely consist of the original text with new headings, though comments and correspondence suggest that additions to up-date the story are likely to be appreciated. These have been supplied where appropriate.

In the original Prelude I confessed that a few years before I would have found it impossible to write about my experience. The time has to be ripe for anyone to go through the process of differentiation and selection required in order to shape the chaos of things into a story. To some extent it happens as one goes along, as memory retains what seems significant and the nitty gritty of life fades into the background. But to order a narrative requires sharper focus, and a process of separating out the strands and discerning relationships other than a simple chronological sequence. I knew that to do as I had been asked and write an account of my son Arthur's life would be a problem in itself — the reasons for this will become apparent as the story proceeds. As for my response to it, it was and is so bound up with everything else, my total theological pilgrimage, even my decision to seek ordination as a Methodist minister. As I expected, the story became a kind of personal testimony.

But I recognised that the effect of personal testimony is all too often to distract attention from God to oneself, and the effect of separating things out into different chapters was to tear them apart until it almost seemed as though God was just one element alongside other elements in the picture. So right at the start I tried to get the balance right. From the perspective from which I wrote, I could only look back on all that had happened with a sense of gratitude and an awareness of the grace of providence. Somehow God seemed behind and before everything.

I knew it seemed terribly presumptuous to think like that, and yet it is there in the Bible; whether you look at Jeremiah, or the Psalms, or Paul, you find that sense that somehow God had known, consecrated and appointed even before birth, a sense of destiny. It seems as if it is only hindsight that permits one to see things in this light, to discover that everything is integrated together, to see that God was there

3

all the time and that there is no way he is merely one aspect
of experience. It seems as if it is only the language of the
Bible that can capture this perspective. So I began with a
Psalm of Testimony: .

I will exalt you, O Lord,
  for you have drawn me up from the depths,
    and have not suffered hopelessness to triumph over me.

O Lord my God, I cried out in my emptiness,
  and you have made me whole.

You brought me back from the wilderness places,
  you saved my life from among those who know you not.

Sing praises to the Lord, all you his faithful ones,
  and give thanks to his holy name.

Gracious and righteous is the Lord,
  full of compassion is our God.

For you, O Lord, delivered my soul from the shadow,
  my eyes from tears and my feet from falling.

So I will walk before the Lord
  in the land of the faithful.

I believed I was lost,
  I was brought very low,
    I said in my haste: there is no God.

The Lord tested me,
  he tested my mind,
    he tested my heart.

When I was a student, I thought I should be a minister,
  but I was a woman and the door was then shut.

4

Nonetheless I went on to study the scriptures,
  to seek knowledge of the things of God,
    convinced I had to, in spite of the barriers.

But the Lord drove me into the wilderness
  and hid his face from me.

Vainly I cried out, What is your will, O God?

The Lord afflicted me,
  he made me taste the waters of bitterness, creation's sadness;
    my first-born was handicapped.

Vainly I cried out, Why, O God, have you deserted us?

The Lord showed me all the wickedness of the heart,
  all the injustice in the world,
    all the warfare of humanity.

Vainly I cried out, Where, O God, shall we find you?

In despair I said,
  either God is a demon,
    or there is no God.

But the Lord took pity on me,
  he heard my cry.

In the inner depths of my mind,
  I heard a voice:

I am the Lord,
  believe in me or not —
    it makes no difference to *me.*

Then I knew it was the Lord,
  and my heart was humbled.

As I journeyed on my way,
  again he spoke to me:

Go, teach and preach,
  be my minister.

For this I prepared you from birth,
  for this I led you through the wilderness,
    for this I am setting you on your feet
      and putting my joy and love within your heart.

Then my heart leapt within me,
  and my being was filled with song:

O give thanks to the Lord for he is good,
  for his mercy endures for ever.

But who am I that I should serve him thus?
  The tempter spoke of pride.
    The call of the Lord I hid within myself.

But in due time the Lord opened the doors,
  and gave me the conviction to press on along the way.

He made the teacher a preacher,
  he made the lost sheep a shepherd,
    he nurtured things in me I'd never known were there.

He put words in my mouth
  and prayers on my lips
    and love in my heart.

He shaped my ministry,
  he took up into my ministry the whole of my past,
    my studies and my sufferings — even my handicapped son.

So the questionings of my heart were stilled,
  the doubts of my mind were silenced.

The Lord has shown me what is his will
  and so I declare it to you.

How then shall I repay the Lord for all his benefits to me?

I will take the cup of salvation
and call upon the name of the Lord.

O Lord I am your servant,
your servant and the descendant of your servants;
You have unloosed my bonds.

I will offer you a sacrifice of thanksgiving.
and call upon the name of the Lord.

I will pay my vows to the Lord
in the presence of all his people

in the courts of the house of the Lord,
even in the midst of the congregation.

Praise the Lord with me.[1]

1 This composition is indebted to the *Alternative Service Book* version of Psalms
30 and 116

Chapter 1

HOPE THEN — WHAT NOW?

When Arthur was twenty-one, we made no attempt to give him a latch-key. He needs help to get through the door. But he goes out to work every day and earns a little pocket-money, known as 'wages', at an Adult Training Centre. He has something of a life of his own, and spends ten–twelve weeks a year away from home, on holiday with the Catholic Handicapped Children's Fellowship, or a week at a time at the local Short Stay Relief ward. He draws an Invalidity Pension and Mobility Allowance, though actually as his Mum I have to do it all — he cannot talk let alone sign his name.

It was in 1984 that I wrote Arthur's story, and I began by describing a day in his life. Little has changed, except that he has moved on from school and the children's hostel where he used to stay. We can begin there, and then add a few up-dating paragraphs.

A Day in 1984

I begin to write on 26 March 1984. Last night my son, Arthur, really did stand unsupported for a few seconds. He has been getting nearer and nearer to it for the past year or so. There's still a long way to go, but still, for once we can date a moment of achievement.

But let's face the facts. Arthur was born on 1 June 1967; so he is rising seventeen. He was standing leaning against the bedroom wall as I put on his nappy, and pulled up his plastic pants and pyjama trousers. Yes. We have been washing nappies for nearly seventeen years. That is the sort of reason why this can hardly be the story of Arthur's life.

His life lacks event. It is a kind of slow motion in which all track of time goes lost. We know our family is growing up and we are getting older, not through our eldest son, but our second. Edward, though two years younger, is 'big brother' in our family. Arthur is in size no bigger than William, our nine-year-old, and in development not even a toddler. So there is hardly a biography to be written. It is easier to start with Arthur as he is now, and trace some of the things that have contributed to the present situation.

Arthur's day begins when the bedcovers are turned back and he is roused from sweet dreams by having his leg splints removed. Oh the relief expressed in his stretch, and then the delighted curl up! He snuggles up and prepares to drop off again. At the weekend he often gets away with it, but on school days there will only be ten minutes' comfort before the next interruption.

Every night he sleeps in splints to keep his legs straight — or at least, as straight as they can go. The splints are quite easy to manipulate. They are moulded to his legs, each one different, and held in place by velcro straps. They go over his pyjamas because we found they were causing eczema when next to his skin. Luckily he has very little skin trouble now, but one 'event' in his life was a period of weeks in hospital when infected eczema spread all over his body. That was when he was about twenty months old. But back to the splints — about two years ago both his legs were in plaster. The problem was that having learned to crawl at about the age of four, he sat on his heels for ten years or more, always on the floor where he did at least have some mobility. Gradually the tendons in his knees contracted, because his legs were never straight. For years we had 'walked him' around ourselves when getting him from one place to another, but as his legs got more and more bent he became less and less willing to take his weight on them.

Medical advisers began to feel something should be done, partly because he showed signs of acquiring more balance and there was some hope he might begin to get on his feet if it were physically more comfortable, partly because they feared progressive contraction until his legs were so bent he would become extremely difficult to handle. So after much heartsearching, we agreed to experiment with serial plasters. What this meant was putting his legs in plaster as straight as possible, and then gradually forcing the plasters straight with wedges behind his knees. It was a long drawn out process. We were very apprehensive because Arthur has never been one to take discomfort in his stride. He has always tended to over-react physically and emotionally, whether to cold, infection or any other problem. But we survived various ups and downs, and now we know it was all worth it. Neither leg is quite straight even now, and we have to make sure his legs are kept as straight as possible during the night to prevent reversion. But last night he did maintain a precarious balance for a few seconds. Every night he uses the double rail on the stairs and walks himself up without assistance. At school he gets around on a 'walker'. With someone to hold his hands, he walks down the drive to his school 'bus' every morning. It was really worth it.

But it is only hindsight that has given us that assurance. One of the most difficult things has been deciding what is for the best. I vividly remember the first weekend he was in plaster. He had a bit of a cold and it went to his chest. He was certainly ill. But somehow it seemed more than the illness warranted. He just contracted out completely, and slept and slept. But when he got over the feverish cold, a remarkable thing had happened. He had adjusted to the plasters. He accepted his immobility without complaint. Gradually he learned to sit on the floor with his legs out in front of him — in other words it increased his balance on his bottom which had never been much good. Then he learned to swing his legs around plaster and all, and to shuffle on his bottom. We had never dreamed he could learn new motions so quickly, since he had been stuck in the same motions for years.

But that was not the end of trouble, after all. Six weeks later, and a little while after the plasters had been changed, we had a traumatic weekend. He cried and cried. He could not sleep. We could not comfort him. Eventually the plasters were removed, and on his heels were dreadful pressure sores. So there were weeks of delay while the sores healed. It was to happen again — just as the physiotherapist was crowing with delight that his legs were almost straight, his distress returned. At least that time we knew what it was and we were able to take prompt action.

Of course having both his legs in plaster also complicated life at the practical level. He had to be carried upstairs and was a lot heavier and more awkward than usual. He could not be bathed, which, for a child in nappies with a tendency to skin trouble, was quite a problem. But such difficulties were nothing compared with coping with his distress. I was most grateful that I did not usually have to take him to the hospital and join the gang of nurses holding him down as he struggled against the plastering. The problems were multiplied by the fact that we could not communicate to him what was happening or why, nor could he communicate to us the cause of his distress.

But still it has been worth it. Last night he stood unsupported for a few seconds. So even though I know he would rather sleep without his splints, all curled up like anyone else, I know it is best to persevere. And his day begins with the removal of the splints.

Ten minutes or so later, in comes a spoonful of jam containing four pills, three of them very large, and the poor child has these thrust into his mouth, willy nilly. It is quite something to swallow those things, but the jam provides some sweet lubrication.

One of the first things I asked when told that Arthur was handicapped was would he develop fits. The specialist thought not. Some months later we were staying with my parents in Belfast, and we discovered him in a strange sort of coma, not breathing properly, going purple. I cannot remember the exact sequence of events after all these years, but we ended up in hospital — both of us, since I was able to stay in with him. What had happened was that he had gone into *status epilepticus*, a state of continuous fitting. As a result he was deprived of oxygen — hence the purple. The danger was more brain damage. Happily once out of it, he recovered and was soon out of hospital. But from that day till now he has taken drugs to prevent epileptic fits. In fact the fits have not been as much of a problem as they can be for many. For most of his childhood they have been under control except when he was sickening for a fever. Then the first sign of infection would be a major fit, and as he came round he would begin to get hot. The last few years the pattern has changed, and it has been a bit difficult to predict or prevent the fits. There was one frightening evening when I left him as usual sitting in the bath while I got on with other odd jobs upstairs. After a short time I sensed something was wrong — I suppose it had been unusually quiet or something; you can usually hear him making noises of some sort. As I went into the bathroom he began to sputter. He was flat on his back, almost under water, and just coming round from a fit. That was the worst moment of several months when quite serious fits could occur weekly or fortnightly. His medication has been increased, but the problem is not entirely solved. However, we think now — and his school teachers agree — that there is a connection between the fits and constipation. So we have been experimenting with his diet to try and sort that one out — not easy, since he has never been a very willing eater.

Interestingly, Arthur always seems to have known that the pills mattered. There have been times when he has been ill and refused all food and drink — but he has still taken his drugs. Occasionally if he is in a mischievous mood, he will grin with his teeth firmly clenched, eyes twinkling, and it all becomes a game. But in the end he always co-operates with his drugs, if nothing else.

He usually gets a few minutes more in bed to make sure the pills have gone down. Then he is dressed. It was more difficult when our other boys were younger. Having two to dress when we all had to get out of the house in the morning was a bit hectic. But now we have settled into a routine where my husband, Bob, cooks the breakfast while I dress Arthur — and the others fend for themselves. Dressing Arthur is a process that has evolved over the years. He used to sleep in a cot — in fact it is not much more than three years since he transferred into a bed. We had a slightly large-sized cot and he was always curled up anyway. Besides, he used to get himself down off a sofa or bed, preferring to be on the floor where he could crawl or sit on his heels. Then came the decision to straighten his legs, and knowing he would not then be able to use the cot, we began the transfer some months in advance, especially since it made it easier for the school to take him away to a seaside educational centre for a week. Anyway, in those cot days I used to dress him on my knee, and we had a changing table on which to lie him to change his nappies. It got more and more awkward as he got longer. Things are easier now. I change him lying in bed in the mornings. Then his trousers are pulled on and he helps by lifting up his bottom as I pull them up. After putting on shoes and socks, for which he will lift each foot in turn anticipating what I shall do, his legs are swung down and he sits on the bed while his top end is dressed. Here we have recently made a bit of progress. If his pyjama top, or a shirt or jumper, is eased up his back and over his elbows, he can get it off over his head and pull the sleeves off his arms. It is important to make him do what he can, even if it is quicker to do it oneself. But sometimes one just does not realize that he could, and it comes as a great surprise to discover his new capabilities. One just gets into habits, and he does too. Sometimes it is someone else who makes the breakthrough, like the time when my mother discovered the easiest way to change his nappy was to stand him up against something rather than lying him on a nappy changer. That really eased our arrangements downstairs.

So on go vest, T-shirt and jumper, usually a clean one every day, since dribbling is still a bit of a problem. For ages he has pushed his arms through sleeves, but otherwise I still do it all while he sits on the side of the bed. Then I stand him up, and he holds me round the waist while I tuck everything into his trousers and pull down his jumper. Then I take his hands and we proceed like a dancing couple, me going backwards, out of the bedroom, across the landing and down the two top stairs. Then we have reached the long flight with the hand rails and I am able to go down in front while he walks down with one hand on one rail, the other on my shoulder. Thank goodness the days of carrying downstairs are over.

Meanwhile breakfast is on the table. Arthur has his own menu these days — Weetabix, All-bran and prunes! Feeding has been an intermittent problem all his life, and between us we have unfortunately set up behaviour patterns which are frustrating and difficult to break. He is liable to refuse to take the first mouthful of anything on

14

principle. Sometimes he will simply hold out until everyone else has finished and then decide to eat. Sometimes I lose patience long before that, and we have a physical tussle to get the first mouthful in. Usually I win, and once he has taken that first mouthful he will go on to eat willingly. Refusal after the first mouthful I usually accept — then he really does mean 'no'. Frustrating as it is, the first mouthful problem probably shows that he has some capacity to learn from experience: there have been odd occasions when I have inadvertently popped in a mouthful that was too hot. And there are some signs that we are at last growing through this behaviour pattern. I guess really I ought to start being consistent about taking no for an answer, and then he would learn that if he wants food he has to take it willingly first go. But when you are in a hurry to get everyone off to school, and you are afraid he will get into difficulties if he misses his prunes, it is not as easy as all that.

I have long since given up worrying when he fails to eat or drink, but behind the tussle over the first mouthful there is certainly a long-standing problem. If you can get on the wrong foot with a normal child, you can even more with a handicapped child, and build up behaviour patterns that go on for years. I remember being delighted when Arthur started throwing things on the floor — after all it is a normal stage of development for a baby to throw toys out of a pram. But ten years and several broken plates later, one is not so delighted. I remember actually teaching him to take my spectacles off! For some time I have been trying to undo that mistake. And as for the feeding and drinking — well, he was born premature weight though full term, and everyone kept on about his weight when he was a baby, assuming he had to make up ground. He was a very disturbed baby, and everyone assumes that a disturbed baby is a hungry baby. He was a very difficult baby to feed, even

15

after we abandoned trying to breast feed. He would suck down a bottleful and then suddenly regurgitate the whole lot (I shall never forget the time my great aunt wanted to feed the baby, would not be dissuaded — and ended up with the whole feed all over her lap). We battled on, unaware at that stage that there was anything wrong with him, and with intermittent and not always helpful advice from health visitors and clinics. I became Dr Spock's[2] 'anxious giantess' struggling to get food and drink into a reluctant Arthur. The roots of the problem with drink are even clearer. I never succeeded in weaning him off the bottle on to a cup, try as I would. At the age of four he still had most of his liquid in a bottle, and sucked a bottle to settle to sleep every night. Then one day the specialist said that I must withdraw the bottle. He would never acquire the right facial muscles for speech if he was still sucking. So I withdrew the bottle. And Arthur has had a problem with drink ever since, refusing to drink when he is away from home, refusing to drink if there is anything unusual, just refusing to drink. And sometimes even now I see him sucking away in his sleep.

Arthur has never learned to feed himself, though I suspect he does do more at school. Encouraged by various professionals, we have from time to time made an effort to get him to hold a spoon. We have obtained specially designed dishes from which it is possible to scoop food very easily. But somehow resolutions to try and teach him to feed himself always seem to break down. It is partly that it is so much easier just to feed him, and surrounded by so many pressures one takes the easier way out. (I know professionals will heave a sigh about the inadequacies of parents on reading this, but what is the point in concealing the realities?) More fundamental, however, is the counter-productive effect of

[2]   Dr Benjamin Spock, *Baby and Child Care*, New English Library 1966.

trying to drive him. We stimulated in him a very determined streak by our early efforts to get him mobile — at one time a physiotherapist came to work with him once a week, but she eventually gave up because he became so resistant to it. Arthur does not want to be pushed, and he certainly lets us know it. This makes one wonder how wise it is to persist when he refuses to co-operate. Besides, the fact is that the long periods when he is 'off his food' and unco-operative are so profoundly discouraging. Instead of grabbing everything and putting it into his mouth like a normal baby, he has to be wheedled and coaxed, and often would prefer not to know. There is no instinctive interest on which to build. The only thing he has ever put in his own mouth is his thumb. And you cannot even interest him in picking up sweets and putting them in his mouth, since anything the slightest bit hard — even a Smartie — he will push out of his mouth with his tongue rather than eat. (It really *is* remarkable that he swallows those pills!) When he is in the right mood and encouraged in the right way, he can get a loaded spoon to his mouth now. But, without constant watching, any plate or spoon left in his reach will land on the floor. The gains in this area have been exceedingly slight over years of trying.

So in the morning I feed him — while chivying the others to get off to school! He takes a long time over it, even though his breakfast is soggy and needs little chewing. With luck he has finished, been tidied up and had his coat put on by the time the school transport arrives. Then off he goes with his bag of nappies and other necessities.

Arthur has been at the same school since he was five. There have been changes of teachers and classrooms, but no bigger changes than that. We were very lucky. Just as he reached the age of five, the former Training Centres were transferred from Social Services to Education, those over school leaving age moved on, and places were made available for five year olds where previously children often had to wait until they were eight before getting a place. Now we are lucky again. In the last few years it has been accepted that the education act means that if parents desire it and the school agrees that a child may benefit, that child has the right to education up to the age of eighteen. We thought Arthur would have to leave last year, but he is still attending the same school and will for another year.

At school he is helped with mobility, toiletting, feeding and other basic self-help skills, as well as doing educational things similar to those most children do in nursery school or play group. During the last few years the school has organized the plastering and physiotherapy which has had such a marked effect on his progress through liaison with a school for the physically handicapped. Some of the children at Arthur's school are capable of simple reading, but for most of them it is education into socially acceptable behaviour and self-help that is most important. Many of them make their way to school by public transport under the eye of 'guides', but transport is provided for the very young and those whose handicap includes physical disabilities. Arthur has been picked up at the gate for many years now, though we used to take and fetch him for the first year or two. One thing that dictates our day is ensuring that there is someone at home by 3.30 p.m. to meet him when he returns. Until four years ago my mother-in-law lived with us, so there was always 'Nanny'; more recently we have appreciated the reliability of Mrs Walsh who comes three afternoons a week and keeps the household on an even keel. Working mums always have conflicts of duty; with a handicapped child they do not ease off with the passing of years.

When he gets home Arthur often spends a little time on

his roundabout. This was made out of an old Bendix washing machine — the drum forms a base, and the screw which once spun the drum round allows the top to rotate as he pushes himself around with his feet. He can sit in the hall at the centre of the house and swing round watching all the comings and goings. As he does so he will 'purr' away to himself, or come out with his half dozen 'words'. He will clap his hands or gaze at the light coming through the fancy glass windows of the hall between his moving fingers. Watching his fingers is an old, old habit going right back into babyhood. My grandmother taught him to clap his hands when he was about two. Old behaviour patterns survive even as new ones appear. We first noticed an attempt to copy a word when he was about seven. He always liked to watch trees, and out in his pushchair one day, he responded to 'trees' with 'eeesh'. Since then he has acquired 'har' (= car), shoo, you, chair, orr (more), 'hime' (= time), er oo are (here you are), and other even more marginal attempts. The most consistent and long-standing is his own name, 'Aa-er', with the right intonation. This soon became 'uh-oo Aa-er' (= Hullo Arthur), proclaimed loudly as he entered school, and on many other occasions — after all, it was what everyone said to him, so he said it back. This has undergone further developments: we have often called him A.T. or Arthur T. (the T standing for his second name, Thomas), and he has adopted Aa-er T., Aa T. and even Aa-fer. These attempts at language are no more than imitative, we think; though sometimes he comes out with the right word in the right context, and we wonder. He seems to understand a firm 'no', and he certainly responds to words and actions which fit his routine, like 'dinner' or 'upstairs'; but probably that is because they fit with habit. Or do we underestimate him? It is hard to tell. I'm pretty sure he recognizes 'garden'.

Arthur has a marvellous sense of humour and will get into infectious fits of giggles. One favourite game has been crouching at the bottom of the stairs watching a ball bounce down every step — not so easy now he does not squat on his heels and his legs have grown longer. It used to be a marvellous way of involving all the family in a game with Arthur — with fielders upstairs, fielders downstairs, etc. Another favourite is to make a paper hat out of newspaper and pull it right over his face. He will pull it off with a smile, or if you crackle the paper before he manages to get it off, great muffled chuckles will rise from within. If he is sitting in a chair and you throw a soft ball on his knee, he will catch it and send it back. Even more fun is slinging a rattle around. Unfortunately his fun-slinging is not confined to acceptable games, however. You should hear his giggles of delight when he gets his plate of dinner on the floor, and even louder giggles when you tell him off! I sometimes feel he has more idea what is going on than we realize!

Arthur enjoys a romp, tickling, being bounced on someone's knee. He loves music of any kind, and watches television. When I take him to church he is quiet all through the hymns, listening and smiling, and then starts vocalizing in the prayers, occasionally picking up the last word of a sentence and copying it. That is his way of participation! In many ways his enjoyments and responses are those of a toddler, and if you get down to that level you can have great fun. But it takes a lot of energy. Happily he is content to sit on his own most of the time. In fact he has always tended to live in a world of his own from which it was necessary to jog him to get any response at all. Now, however, he is much more aware of his environment. He will hear a door open and crane round to see what's happening. He will watch other people's movements. He will even watch the cat, whereas once he seemed totally unaware of his existence, even when the cat rubbed against him. Only the other day I caught him staring into the shaving mirror at himself as he stood against the washbasin in the bathroom. Now that we really do have eye contact with him, we realize how little we had before.

Children's television programmes dominate life between school and dinner. As soon as William arrives home from primary school, Arthur joins him in watching. At 6.0 p.m., most evenings, we congregate in the kitchen for family dinner. Arthur wears a gay PVC overall (the latest came from the National Trust) and sits at his own end of the table. We have a kind of special extension for him which was once a wash-stand with a marble top. At one stage in his life he used to hammer the table with both hands, making a terrible noise and setting the plates bouncing. Tired nerves could not stand it. Nor could we keep everything out of his reach. He cannot make the marble bounce, and we keep everything off his area. But he sits up on an ordinary chair and joins the family meal. I can just reach to feed him. Arthur's presence has made it difficult to instil formal table manners into the other children, and family meals tend to be a bit of a riot. Arthur is so slow, we have had to allow the others to get down for an intermission between dinner and dessert. But as they grow older and more self-conscious, it is clear that they can behave at table when we have visitors. Maybe our relaxed regime is not too damaging after all.

Arthur now stays up for most of the evening. Music practice and homework dominate the house and he usually has to amuse himself. He will often crawl into the back room to listen to the music, usually taking his favourite plastic 'hammer' with him. This is a rattle to which he has been attached for years. He has developed a most remarkable range of hand and wrist movements with it, and the sound seems to please him. He has had a long succession of them — they do tend to get brittle in time and crack and lose the beads. Unfortunately this makes them unsafe for young children, so they have become almost impossible to obtain. But so far we have managed to acquire enough to keep him going. Round about 9.30 or so, we will start him upstairs for his bath. Physically speaking the bathing is the most difficult stage of the day for us. Once undressed he has to be lifted in, and, what is worse for the back, lifted out. A chair by the bath helps. He sits on it and we swing him in from it, reversing the process when we get him out. It is lucky he is so small for his age. Arthur has never liked putting bare feet to the ground. His soles have never hardened off since he has never run around enough. But he has now learned to grip his arms round my neck, so I can more easily lift him from the chair and carry him to bed. He sits on the bed to have his pyjamas on, though I stand him against the wall to put on the nappy and pull up his pants and trousers — and that's where we began. There are still his splints to put on and his drugs to give him. Then he is tucked up and wished goodnight. Usually there is nothing more to do till next morning.

This 'Day in the Life of Arthur' has introduced most of the facts about his incapacity, how we cope and how we got here. He was born brain-damaged, microcephalic (that is, with an abnormally small head), as a result of a placenta which was too small and inefficient, depriving him of necessary oxygen during his development in the womb, a full-term baby but premature weight. Nothing more by way of cause can be traced, in spite of many tests. Brain cells do not repair, though work with stroke victims has shown that undamaged cells can learn to compensate. So programmes for handicapped children are often geared to establishing activities which the child would not progress to unaided. We were taught 'patterning' when Arthur was about eighteen months, a method of moving arms and legs back and forth in the crawling pattern. It was believed that this could stimulate development over a very broad front. In fact it meant he crawled long before he developed the balance to sit unsupported, and although he sometimes enjoyed the motion for motion's sake, haring across a room at a kind of canter, it did not have any other beneficial effect. He was unable to take in the presence of a favourite toy on the other side of the room and go and fetch it, for example. His ability to manipulate toys has always been very limited indeed. When he was in a cot, he had a musical box hung on the side, and he was able to catch his fingers in a fairly capacious handle device and pull the string to wind the music up. We always knew when Arthur was awake! But he has never learned to produce sound from other play devices, and apart from the favourite rattles and balls, little else has caught on. He is a very difficult child to buy Christmas and birthday presents for.

He has at times been a difficult child to take anywhere. There were a number of years when he got very distressed at being in strange places. I remember a disastrous holiday in the Lake District. It would have been a nice cottage, if it had not rained all the time, and my parents' car had not broken down on the motorway, and Arthur had not refused to sleep or eat or co-operate with anything, moaning and mizzling away, getting worse and worse for lack of sleep, only happy in the familiar environment of the family car — so we drove round in the rain for four days and then gave up and came home. He could cause problems even when reasonably happy by letting out ear-piercing screams, mostly because he liked the sound — but it is not easy to contain this sort of thing in a public place. Even at toddler age he could create unbearable tension simply because he had no interest in the world around him and so tended to cry at physical discomfort for hours — like the occasion we went for a walk in the country with him in a backpack, and he howled for an hour or more.

On the other hand, as long as we had other babies and toddlers in pushchairs, Arthur too could be coped with, and usually he survived local walks and weeks at the seaside, even enjoying watching trees and feeling the breeze on his face. It is a different matter now. We are outdoors people; we were mountaineers in our youth. We prefer camping to hotels, and our growing boys need the experience of walking and cycling and roughing it. So do we, if we are to keep fit and ward off the decline into old age. So for some years now we have had to find alternatives for Arthur's care while taking an activity holiday. Local authority short stay hostels have gradually provided a better and better service. There was a time when the social worker would find places in a different place each year, and it was rather a wrench to abandon Arthur to the unknown. Now, however, he is on the rota for a local hostel which is closely linked with his school. Every month we get a week's relief, including a weekend. We still find ourselves feeling obliged to get out somewhere on those occasions, making the most of opportunities. The arrangement for Arthur is ideal. He attends school every day from the hostel, and is even conveyed in the same transport! We send him off to school on Monday morning, and he returns from school the following Monday. However, there is always pressure on places in the school holidays, understandably, and last year we were very grateful to be able to relinquish any claim to the hostel in August — Arthur went on holiday himself with the Catholic Handicapped Childrens' Society. I was so pleased for him to have the fresh air of the countryside, and the whole experience. He loves being outside in good weather, although his skin is too fair to stand much direct sun. And he loves trips by car or minibus. More and more he looks out of the window and seems to take in something of the environment. The first time I realized he really wanted to walk was one day when the back door was open, and he made a beeline for it, feet outstepping the rest of him — he just wanted to be in the garden after months of winter captivity.

These then are the facts of his life. What of the future? What are his prospects? Clearly he may make some more progress in mobility and self-help skills, but he is going to be dependent all his life. He will need 'special care'. He is so limited that without the family environment he could easily become institutionalized. On the other hand, if he lives at home until we are too doddery to cope any more, the change will be the worse for him. Happily the short term care scheme provides a half way house — until he leaves school. Then there is still a fair amount of uncertainty, and the moment is getting ever closer. Will he get a place in a Training Centre where he would be cared for and trained during the day while still living at home? For the moment that is the solution we would like. We do not think it would be easy to maintain a relationship with him if we were not handling him, living with him. You could not visit him in hospital and maintain a conversation. But if for the moment that seems best, will we get regular short term relief? Provision for adults is woefully limited. We are increasingly aware that the short term relief is what allows us to recoup our energies and have something to give him when he is at home. Absence makes the heart grow fonder. Constant care saps patience. There is no guarantee that the even keel on which we now sail will continue. We have to live with uncertainty. And we have to live without much hope for improvement. As I re-work what I have written two months later, I look back on six weeks of Arthur being unwell with chest infections. He has lost weight — eating has been even more problematical than usual. He has lost ground — even the little achievement reported at the beginning of this chapter has not been repeated. It is always the same — a little triumph is followed by a set-back, and real progress can only be discerned over years.

Those are the facts we have to face, and it is no good being sentimental about it. Arthur is lovable, a source of joy. But it is hard to see any satisfactory future in the long term. But then the past has not been all roses, and we have survived so far. Who knows what the future holds? It is no good worrying about it.

Five Years On

We thought it was really worth it in 1984. As 1989 dawns we are less sure. Arthur has lost ground physically. His legs are not so straight, but worse his back is twisted, and his joints are stiffening up. His ankles are pretty well rigid. His ability to take his own weight, to pull himself upstairs, even to crawl, has gradually been eroded. He is not only tighter, but weaker, and he knows it. He is scared, wants support, and is worried about his lack of balance.

Everything seemed at its peak about the time he left school, and hopes of further progress were high. He gradually learned to crawl again, his thigh muscles redeveloped, and he began to sit on the floor more naturally, it seemed, with his legs folded to one side. It took several years to realise that yet again he was establishing a 'fixed' position which would then 'mould' his body and create further handicap. That's how his back got twisted.

The transfer from school to a local Adult Training Centre was a very happy one. He settled down and seemed more happy and responsive than ever before. At first he had no physiotherapy, and we had no more advice from those who had straightened his legs. We began to fear his legs were showing deterioration. But things improved. A physiotherapist began to attend the Centre. Some hydrotherapy became available. We were assured he still had the flexibility in his knees.

But then the twisted back began to force itself on our attention, and a rearrangement of services meant we were able to make renewed contact with the clinic we had been to before. Little could be done, except pull sad faces and try to come up with ideas to improve his posture. A beanbag chair was one idea. So we got one for him for Christmas. We began to discourage him from sitting on the floor in an effort to prevent further deterioration. But we were in even more of a Catch-22 situation than we realised. The nice relaxing bean bag meant he was not using his muscles to support himself, and the sitting in chairs meant he was not crawling. So little by little he got weaker. It is impossible to know what to do for the best! At least I don't get guilty any more — whatever you do is wrong anyway!

So a year later we have lost even more ground. But the consultant thinks there may be even more to it, that he may be developing a certain spasticity and the problems go back to the brain. We are experimenting with a relaxing drug given to spastics. But we know that a big shift in perspective has had to take place over the past twelve months — we are not going to see improvement, but rather the reverse. What do you do when hope dies? How do you come to terms with deterioration?

Well, you keep trying to carry on with the usual routine, insisting on him doing as much of the old things as possible. You begin to adapt, to think out new ways of coping. If he cannot sit in the bath any more, how can you make it possible for him to lie in it? Why, you pad it with the impervious 'bed-mats' you usually use for lightweight camping, putting a roll under his head and his knees. It is only in minor ways that the routine of 1984 has changed, and a day in the life of Arthur is much the same.

But some new activities have been devised: an old toddlers' play tower has been resurrected and turned into a 'standing-box' (we jokingly refer to it as Arthur's torture-tower) — he copes with about ten minutes in it if you keep him distracted with toys! And that's the real gain, his awareness and response to things. He really looks at things now, responds to a 'Jack-in-a-box', watching with anticipation on his face as his hand is guided to press the release button. He plays ball with cunning and skill, directing it away from the fielders. And he knows he's a monkey! It is simply not possible to leave him on his own for hours any more. He wants company, he wants 'conversation' and laughter and fun. He likes to go out, and clearly loves the ride round in the car that takes him everyday to his Centre. Sometimes we can 'see' him listening to music, his face and response changing markedly as the pace and rhythm changes. We have taken up barn-dancing after years away from it, because Arthur can come along and sit enjoying the music, and the thumping feet, and the noise and activity all around him. It should also help us to keep fit and able to go on handling him. Luckily he is still very small for an adult, a 21 year old in clothes made for a 12-13 year old.

We used to laugh about a TV series about Bagpuss, and I guess most parents of young children would smile wryly too: it always began, 'When Bagpuss wakes up, all his friends and relations wake up too.' We can certainly say, 'When Arthur smiles, all his friends and relations do too.' There is something infectious about his enjoyment and his mischief which continues to delight, despite everything. But we no longer imagine the years of distress belong only to the past.

Chapter 2

IS LOVE ENOUGH?

In the last chapter I tried to present Arthur as objectively as possible. But a person has his being in relation to others, and it is not possible to distinguish the facts from the realities of personal reaction entirely. Even less do the facts constitute the whole picture. Now we had better turn to the subjective side of it all — the effect it has had on me, his mother, and on the rest of the family, our feelings and reactions. In 1989 I recognise that they go on being ambivalent. When I originally wrote in 1984, I thought the years of distress belonged to the past, and I could confidently say it was no good worrying about the future, even though I admitted there had been a time when I could not break the hope-less mood which underlay the whole of life, even as we coped and joked and survived.

Arthur was born in Cambridge. When he was eight months old, our GP sent us to see a specialist at Addenbrook's Hospital. I had become worried about one or two things which by hindsight seem rather trivial. Without telling me the real problem, the GP made his referral.

I arrived and sat in a waiting room with other mums. One woman had a huge inert child lying across her knee. Arthur sat on my knee and appeared to be playing with a rattle. 'At least he is not like that,' I thought to myself, still preoccupied with the trivial worries. I went in to be told essentially that he was; that his development was abnormally slow. It is hard to describe the stunned shock and desolation, the bafflement as to what it all meant, the inability to ask the right questions, to understand, the awful self-control needed to go on through that hospital to the X-ray department without breaking down. The reserve broke as I pushed the pram towards the city centre and met Bob in the street.

Next day I went back to the GP, searching for reassurance, for understanding, only to find that he had suspected it from the first moment he had seen the baby after our return from hospital. He explained that doctors were taught not to tell parents, but to respond to questions; in the post-natal period there is a danger of a mother rejecting the baby, and it is better to wait till bonds are formed. So did it have to be eight months? Did he have to duck the task of telling me and let it all happen so impersonally, without preparation? He had been my doctor when I was a student. Did he not realize that he was dealing with an intelligent and self-sufficient person who had struggled for months rather than run for help? Could he not trust himself to handle it? Should he not have insisted on doing regular check-ups and assessment if he had had those suspicions all along? I felt increasingly angry and let down. Doctors pay dearly for losing a patient's trust.

I went to the clinic and saw the doctor there. She had in fact been in closer touch with us than the GP. She too had known for months. Why did she not tell us? It became apparent that she had tried to drop hints. But in the end the buck had been passed. Who was responsible, her or the GP?

I now recognize that there are no parents of handicapped children who have 'good' experiences of being told. It is so traumatic that there is bound to be anger and let down and resentment. But even in a calmer frame of mind, I feel that the professional people handling this sort of thing, need to consider very carefully the policies they have adopted. Of course people are very different. We expected to cope with our baby. We read Dr Spock who reassuringly insists that some perfectly normal babies do not sit up till nine months — no doubt with the worriers in mind. I can see now that over months of real struggle and worry, we suppressed our anxieties, telling ourselves that babies were much more difficult than we had realized, refusing to admit our own incompetence, and as new parents without any previous experience by which to judge the situation, remaining blissfully unaware of the seriousness of our baby's condition. We needed support we did not get (even the health visitor left to get married and was not replaced). We needed information we were not given. Someone should have gently pointed out the significance of the fact that he did not smile until thirteen weeks. Whenever the news came it would have been painful, but we might have managed much better if we had understood the problem, and the shock need not have been so dramatic after so many months. Had he been our second baby I would have known there was something wrong almost from the start, like the doctors.

Nothing went really well from birth, though I had a marvellous pregnancy, remaining very fit right up to the end. A week or two before the birth, the midwife commented that I was lucky because the baby was small, and it would make the first labour easier. That was the first hint of something wrong, had we recognized it — and if we ignore another strange fact: I had always intended to call my first boy Richard, after a brother who died of Hodgkins Disease at the age of sixteen. During my pregnancy I recalled my mother telling me how upset her aunt had been when they gave that name to their baby — she had just lost her son Richard in the Second World War. I panicked. If anything happened to my baby and I had called him Richard, I felt I could never forgive myself. So we agreed on Arthur instead. Was it a strange premonition?

The easy labour did not materialize. I was booked for a home delivery and everything seemed set fair. Five days before the date due, the waters broke in the middle of the night (a few hours after returning from the theatre — I am glad it did not happen there!). We set the wheels in motion. By next morning, however, labour had not established itself, and what contractions there were, ceased. The GP was called in because the discharge was discoloured. He explained that this meant the baby was passing bowel motions and was distressed. I was rushed to hospital. There labour was re-established with a drip stimulant, and by the early evening Arthur was born. At just over five pounds, he was put straight into an incubator for the first couple of days of his life.

It is a strange experience being in a ward with new mums and not having a baby. But my morale was high. I wanted to breast feed, but for the moment could not; so at feeding times I milked myself with a special milking machine, producing enough for all the babies in the premature baby ward. I felt a certain pride in this, though jokingly talked of being a prize cow. Meanwhile Arthur was fed my milk from a bottle. When he eventually came to me, he had no idea what to do with a breast. That was the first of many emotional traumas. The nurses showed me how to use a nipple shield, so he sucked on the familiar teat but took milk from the breast. That is how we managed for weeks. But clearly the effort for him was too much. He had to suck extra hard to stimulate the breast and then was too exhausted to feed. Feeding times were long drawn out and terribly frequent, day and night. After weeks and weeks of trying he eventually learned to take the breast. But that only lasted for a short time. He began to come off it screaming, unable to feed as the milk spurted out. In desperation I abandoned breast feeding. A couple of weeks later he cut two teeth, ridiculously early. That soothed my emotions — I had felt so rejected, but now there was an explanation. Years later, I suspect the problem was his inability to cope with the abundant flow of milk. Nor, as we have seen, did changing to the bottle solve our feeding problems. What it did mean was that some of the pressure could be shared with Bob.

Looking back, Arthur's slowness to learn to take the breast after feeding from a bottle was the first concrete sign. But not knowing his condition, it was something that hurt me deeply at a very instinctive level. After a birth the mother is emotionally volatile — that is well known. The craving for the mutual enjoyment of breast feeding, the sense of rejection when my baby did not enjoy it, just increased the natural feelings of depression and even blinded me to all the signs of love and support that Bob constantly gave. Adjustment to the new member of the family was not easy, whether you consider the practical level, the incessant demands, the time-consuming care, or the more personal and emotional level. I still think that if we had known, some of these pressures would have been eased. I would have understood the feeding problem. We could have given up the attempt to breast feed. We could have accepted he did not need all that feed to catch up with normal babies. No doubt the knowledge of our problems would have hurt, but it would have been a different hurt and a more realistic one.

When the full nature of his problems was revealed, shock, puzzlement and some anger were the first reactions. But it all soon turned into a dreadful sense of failure. Unfortunately about the same time I had been exploring the possibility of some part-time teaching at Birmingham University to which Bob was soon to move. And I received a letter indicating that there was not much opportunity after all. I remember going for a walk on the Gog Magog hills with a friend and being overwhelmed by the sense that I had failed in every aspect of my life — there seemed no career prospects and I had failed as a mother. The future looked bleak. As it has turned out I had no need to feel like that, and looking back it seems a bit over-dramatized. But it was real at the time, and that sense of failure remained submerged until I had successfully produced a normal baby.

Yet, on the whole, after the initial shock, during the early years with Arthur I was relatively adjusted and able to accept the situation. At first it was difficult not knowing what it meant and not being able to find out. No one could really gauge how handicapped he was, or what his future development would be. Consciously or unconsciously all parents have dreams for their children. We had to accept we could dream no dreams. We began to reflect on how important it is to let children develop their own lives, how damaging parental expectations can be. Of course, parents' expectations may provide an essential stimulus to a child to do his or her best, but equally they may have an adverse effect. One need only think of John Betjeman's experience, so compellingly recaptured in *Summoned by Bells*[3]. We thought we had learned from Arthur just to want our children to develop to their greatest potential, no matter how little that proved to be. The truth is we cannot help being just like other parents when it comes to our two normal children: we have ambitions for them, and delight in their talents and their successes. I just hope that we do not impose undue pressure on them. Theoretically at least we recognize that it is of fundamental importance to allow a child the freedom to develop his own unique capacities, to be himself and find his own future. But in Arthur's case, having perforce dropped the natural dreams, other dreams obtruded themselves.

With Arthur, I thought, I shall never have to face the growing up and growing away which is so difficult in the

[3] John Betjeman, *Summoned by Bells*, John Murray 1960.

parent-child relationship. He would always need me. The possessiveness of a mother's love was able to take free play, and with it the tendency to overprotect, inability to accept that anyone else could do for Arthur what I could do. In the initial stages I am sure this was healthy. It was a positive way of coming to terms with the situation. It gave me a purpose, a future, in relation to him. It eased the pain and made me believe I had accepted him, handicap and all. For the early years it was all right. But it had hidden dangers which bore fruit later.

Of course this did not mean that moments of distress did not surface at surprising moments and in surprising ways. I remember watching a mother driven scatty by her child in a supermarket and thinking, 'If she knew what it was like to have a handicapped child she wouldn't treat her child that way.' But a few years later I too was driven scatty by the antics of normal toddlers, and ate my words. Only in the last few years have I been able to get cross with Arthur. I reckon that ability is a sign of a more healthy relationship.

The early months in Cambridge are a blurred memory of pain, of positive acceptance, of sharing with our 'child minder' who was a remarkable support. She, like the doctors, had known there was something wrong from the moment she had met Arthur. But it made no difference to her acceptance of him into her family for the half-days I spent continuing my research. She was the one who opened my eyes to the love I could not see. But compared with Birmingham, the Cambridge days were days of isolation with a problem peculiar to ourselves. Immediately upon arriving in Birmingham, when Arthur was fifteen months old, the health visitor was on our doorstep, and we were introduced to a local 'mums and toddlers' group for handi-capped children. From there we moved on to membership of the Birmingham Society for Mentally Handicapped

Children (now known as Birmingham Mencap). It is impossible to quantify what all that meant to me — just meeting other mums with the same problem, seeing one sweet Irish woman with a spastic almost as big as herself, a huge family, ill-health with asthma — yet she was so cheerful, so full of a simple faith in God, in life. I recognized we were not so badly off, treasured the very real joy I had in Arthur by this time, accepted there was still hope. There too we had our first positive help: Arthur was given regular physiotherapy; ways of stimulating him were discussed. Over the pre-school years, the Society's playgroup was a life-line.

By this time Arthur was through the worst of the babyhood problems, and things seemed set reasonably fair. We went through the 'I will do anything' syndrome, feeling that any effort to stimulate his development was worth it: we adopted the Doman-Delacato patterning routine with the help of a neighbour, and surrounded him with colour, toys, music, anything and everything to drag him out of his private world into our world and facilitate his response and mobility. We never allowed this entirely to push out the rest of life — I continued part-time research. But we certainly knew something of how obsessive the need to do something about the situation can become. I have since recognized it in many parents. On this drive depends the full-scale Doman-Delacato programme developed by the *Institute for the Achievement of Human Potential* (based in Philadelphia). Armies of friends or relatives are needed who will devote their whole lives to getting the maximum development out of the handicapped child, lives programmed to exercises and stimulation twelve hours a day, no life apart from the all-embracing objective. Probably every parent of a handicapped child has to go through this for a period, but if it goes on indefinitely it is, I am sure, profoundly unhealthy. The mother's singlemindedness really can become an obsession, and the rest of the family suffers. A handicapped child not infrequently contributes to marital breakdown. It is not unknown for the siblings of handicapped children to become delinquent. Is it any wonder? Of course, the child may also become a catalyst for deeper commitment to one another and a growing together through the shared burden — but even then the family needs a shared life and interests apart from the 'problem'.

Tremendous care is needed to ensure that the normal children in the family do not feel neglected. I remember the way Edward, almost exactly two years younger than Arthur, interrupted our great efforts to push Arthur's development forward; as soon as he could crawl he came and butted into every attempt to get Arthur to play or move around. We knew that the development of a destructive jealousy was only too likely, and had to discipline ourselves not to thrust him away, however frustrated we might feel. As he grew older, for all the incipient jealousy at home, we began to notice his protectiveness to Arthur when out and about, and when he started school and his life expanded, all trace of competition with Arthur disappeared. Recently he has confessed when under extreme pressure with homework, exams, etc. that sometimes he wishes he was like Arthur and did not have to do anything — but that is just the sigh of an overworked teenager. We are grateful that something that could have been very damaging has simply had the positive effect of helping us to avoid obsession with the handicapped child's development. No amount of effort can ever make him normal, and even what we did stimulated a certain amount of determined opposition. A relaxed relationship is a far more valuable treasure than achievements as the world measures them. In the 'middle' years perhaps we were a little too inclined to give up; maybe we could have done more, but did not because we overreacted against the 'I will do anything' obsession. But the whole family matters, and everyone has to be given his appropriate value in the total context.

It is the 'middle' years (1974-79) that I remember as the years of real strain and difficulty. It showed up in the little things. We had adopted a policy of living as normal lives as possible, and as long as we were dealing with two toddlers together it did not seem too difficult. In a double pushchair Arthur and Edward looked more or less like twins and our constraints were normal enough for a family with small children. The first time we pushed Arthur out in a wheel-chair remains a sharp memory — the sinking feeling in the stomach, the sensitivity to stares, to what people might be thinking. Of course I did not admit it to anyone, but I guess it was a moment of symbolic importance, a stage in the admission of abnormality. Life could not remain normal. We simply could not insist on taking Arthur everywhere we went, however socially desirable. There were circumstances which increasingly restricted him as the horizons of his brother were widened. Indeed, symbols were to be as nothing compared with the practical realities of a growing handicapped child, and even they are as nothing to the constrictions brought about by unacceptable behaviour, screaming and crying, resistance to handling or comfort. That was the awful thing — the battle of love.

The early years really were not so bad. Occasionally Arthur cried and cried and could not be comforted. His inability to communicate meant that even though he was for the most part content, that dreadful helplessness parents often feel with a crying baby was liable to go on recurring. The more we tried to find out what was wrong and do something about it, the worse he tended to get. It was this, writ large, which began to dog our lives. I can almost date the day it started. I was pregnant with William.

Arthur would soon be seven. I pushed him up to the local shops, as I had done so often before. Suddenly parked outside the bread shop he began to scream and cry. I could do nothing with him.

A little later, following Grandad's death, we took Nanny away for a week's holiday in a guest house at Weston after Easter. It was a very mixed week. Arthur was a struggle, and we could not track down what was upsetting him.

For the next few years there would be periods of acute distress, refusal to co-operate with eating, dressing, changing or anything, inability to sleep, rejection of all handling, comfort or affection. During this period progress seemed to stand still. We were relieved when things were simply bearable: the bad patches were somewhat intermittent, and mostly we were able to maintain the regular routine. The worst feature of it was that when he was distressed, there would be a gradual build up of distress in me, until I could no longer contain my feelings. It was his rejection of comfort, rejection of love and care that hurt; it was the distress for his distress which undermined my ability to cope. There seemed no point in his life. If you put an animal out of his misery on compassionate grounds, why not Arthur?

It was impossible to track down the cause. Everyone engaged in one unhelpful suggestion after another — was it because of the arrival of the new baby? It couldn't be. It had started before William's arrival. Arthur could hardly have been aware of him anyway — he was not even aware of the family cat. Was it because of changes of environment? Certainly he was more distressed in unfamiliar surroundings. We had to bring him home from my parents — they had recently retired and were in a different house. We had to bring him home from that disastrous holiday in the Lakes. Strange places could have been something to do with it, but it was not the whole explanation because there were patches of equal agony at home. Coming home usually eased it, but it did not solve it. The search for explanations, the frustration that he could not explain . . . the strain built up — while at the same time we coped with the early years of another new baby, and both of us doing a full time job. We sought advice from doctors. They had no better answer. For a while he was on even more drugs — sedatives given to schizophrenics, to reduce the nervous tension; but they did not solve the problem. The scared look in his eyes would haunt me. I would grit my teeth and try to ignore his cries as I waited in waiting rooms at hospitals and anywhere else I had to take him, knowing that to try to comfort him would make things worse, suffering the embarrassment of knowing that everyone around could not understand why I was doing nothing about my howling child.

Looking back over the years, and particularly these years of more acute difficulty, I realize that I have discovered how distress can become a kind of prison isolating one from others. As a youngster I had often dreamed of how lovely it would be to be surrounded by sympathy — I would bear anything to enjoy that experience, I thought. But actually when things are wrong, you find many people are embarrassed, or they admire you for being brave, indeed, you expect yourself to be brave. You dare not let yourself down. So there is a mutual conspiracy not to admit your need and sympathy fails to materialize. What sympathy is expressed you cannot cope with. If you break down (and I have on several memorable occasions), you feel awful. The only way to prevent that happening is to withdraw, to suppress your real feelings, to hide your vulnerable self and refuse to acknowledge that there is anything really wrong. You have to put on a public face of triumph over difficulty. So isolation deepens. It is also very difficult to learn to ask for help, or even accept help generously offered. Either requires an admission that you are not self-reliant and omnicompetent, and it is too humiliating. You respond with conventional polite clichés, and keep well-meaning people at arm's length. My experience makes me acutely aware of how hard it is to be on the receiving end. We all imagine that helping people is the demanding thing; but it is far more demanding to receive help with genuine grace and gratitude.

It was during this rough period that we brought ourselves to accept periods of relief arranged by our social worker — just to get a break, a chance to go away and do something different without the strain of Arthur. Every time the wrench was dreadful. I hated parting from him. I still could not believe that anyone else could look after him. If I could not understand, it was even less likely a stranger could. I was guilty at leaving him in one strange place after another with strange people to care for him. I had to steel myself, grit my teeth and run away. Once away it was not so bad. At least being away from home and actively engaged in energetic holidays or trips with our other boys, my mind did not dwell too much on how Arthur was coping, and we all came back to the battle somewhat refreshed. Sometimes I am sure he was genuinely all right; other times I suspected that staff protected me from real knowledge of how he had been.

Those were the years when hopelessness about the future, as well as despair about the present, would easily set in. In the early years we had hoped he would eventually have a life of his own, perhaps in one of the establishments of the Home Farm Trust, who set out to create a worthwhile life for the mentally handicapped. But we began to realize he would never make the grade; he would never be self-sufficient enough in terms of mobility, toiletting, dressing,

etc., let alone ability to contribute to a community like that.
The future seemed totally daunting — institutionalization
for him, either sooner if the strain finally broke us, or later
when we were too old to carry on. Even in times of relative
rationality, there seemed no hope for the future, no possibility of his having a life worth living. I found myself voicing
this in an article which received some circulation among
parents and professionals[4], voicing my protest at the success of antibiotics which kept children like Arthur alive into
adulthood for no reason at all; was there not a moral
difference between killing and letting nature take its
compassionate course? Next time Arthur had a chest infection, why could I not refuse treatment? Society by its
treatment of death as taboo, by the success of modern
medicine, was more cruel than nature — few severely
handicapped people used to live beyond their teens. Was
not quality of life more important than quantity? When I
wrote about quality of life at least one reader thought I
meant quality of *my* life, *our* lives. Heaven forbid! I meant
the quality of Arthur's life. How could we justify his continued misery when the future held nothing for him?

Reactions to this article were interesting: some mothers
wrote expressing profound gratitude that someone had
voiced their feelings; others said, 'Why doesn't she get out
and do something?' as if the deeper questions could be
submerged in a flurry of activism. Perhaps I should stress
that all this happened *before* the widely reported case of Dr
Arthur who was prosecuted by the Life organization for
assisting a handicapped baby to die in peace. At the time I
had respected the wisdom of the doctor who assured me

---

[4] 'Family Forum: What is the purpose of it all?' *Apex*, Journal of the British
Institute of Mental Handicap, Vol. 7, no. 2, 1979, p. 52. Reprinted in the
Yearbook of the Birmingham Society for Mentally Handicapped Children,
1981.

that compassionate judgment was often exercised, and it was better not to make a public issue of it. I was very moved to read that Dr Arthur had his Bible in the dock. I do not think that 'Save life at any price' is an essentially Christian perspective; it is a legalism demanded by those who dare not risk using their own judgment or trusting anyone else to. It is an officious meddling with the Creator's compassionate arrangements. It is the panic reaction of those who cannot face death because they have no hope in God.

Our problem did eventually pass. Progress re-established itself. Maybe it was desperately slow, but over long periods of time it was discernible. I shall never forget the day Arthur crawled across the room and climbed on to my knee — after all those years of refusing my embraces. Nor shall I forget the time he tried to push away his youngest brother in order to have my knee to himself. He still has patches of preferring to be left alone, particularly when he is unwell, but now we can take it in our stride and shrug it off. Maybe it would all have been easier if I had been as relaxed then as I am now.

Arthur began to emerge from the dark tunnel, and his hair to turn curly, when his anti-convulsant was changed to Epilim. He finally put it all behind him after the withdrawal of Phenobarbitone three years later. Doctors say that Phenobarbitone can be an irritant. I am now certain that it aggravated the problem. As usual, however, we are wiser after the event. Looking back it was during this period that he changed his front baby teeth. His adult front teeth are enormous, and because his mouth was slightly misshapen, they did not come through where his baby teeth had been, but cut newly through his front gums. It was not easy to recognize at the time, but his behaviour was not unlike a very exaggerated case of a teething baby. His resistance to feeding and handling may well have arisen from the fact that he was unable to tell us his mouth was sore and he felt rotten. Because we struggled with him (remember we have had long term feeding problems), he got scared of what we were doing to him. Unlike a normal child he got no fun out of loose teeth, and he was not distracted from soreness and discomfort by all the other interests and activities that a growing and maturing child usually has. He was as miserable at eight years old as a baby of five months can be, but the effect was more violent and distressing because he was bigger, and had a nervous irritability associated with his condition, and with the drugs he was taking. This now seems the most plausible explanation.

Why did we not see it at the time? How could we have given him those extra drugs as if he were mentally ill as well as handicapped? I have sometimes looked back and been overwhelmed with guilt. Of course, some will say: parents of handicapped children are usually afflicted with guilt, thinking it is their fault they have a handicapped child. I suspect that many mothers have at some time or other felt a bit like that; certainly I asked myself what I had done wrong during pregnancy. But I do not think parental reactions can be stereotyped in this way. Basically I was satisfied that in human terms it was an accident and not my fault. There was no reason to feel guilty just because my child was handicapped. But I have felt guilty about what I have done to Arthur. I guess I am rather too prone to blame myself and to get guilty about things anyway.

But there have been some things which I have inadvertently done which have affected him badly — even complicated his already difficult situation. It is those things I have felt guilty about, things like giving him those unnecessary and useless drugs all those years — what did they do to him? Particularly distressing have been the physical distortions of his body to which I know I have contributed — all unwittingly at the time. When he was a baby I put him on his tummy to sleep. This was then unusual in Britain, but I had come across it in the States and been convinced that it helped with getting up wind and ensuring more settled sleep. But Arthur never learned to lift his head and turn it. He settled in a comfortable position, always facing the same way, and refusing to be lain the other way. He remained at the little baby stage for months longer than usual, and gradually, from spending most of his life in that position, his head became severely distorted in shape. It has more or less grown right again — only those who know would notice the lop-sidedness that remains. But it was hurtful to look at him and know one's own responsibility for it when he was younger. And the way his legs doubled up — it was I who had encouraged his squatting on his heels, realizing it gave him balance and he could sit up and play with toys, or crawl around. But with his feet turned outwards under him, his legs were in a badly distorted position. Not only did all the tendons contract, but his hips were settling a bit out of joint. Even now the ball does not go properly into the socket in either hip, though happily they are functional. When he was a baby, Arthur used to make himself rigid like all babies do and 'stand' on my knee; when he was toddler age he could pull himself up to standing in a baby walker. Then his legs were beautifully straight. Physically he seemed perfect. Of course much of the wasting of his legs would have happened anyway. His failure to learn to walk inevitably meant his feet and lower leg muscles did not develop normally, unlike his thighs which were strengthened by his years of crawling. Yet I know that I contributed to his problems; all those months in plaster were partly my fault. A physiotherapist had even warned me, but I did not then understand the warning. At that stage the all-important thing seemed to be his mobility, the maximum independence we could encourage — and the place where he could develop that was on the floor, squatting on his heels with his feet turned out.

It is this sort of thing that has made me feel guilty, the things I have actually done wrong. It is my inadequacy as his parent, my unintentional contributions to his difficulties, my inability even now to do for him all they say I could if I put my mind to it. For years I have known I ought to be teaching him to feed himself, I ought to be regularly toiletting him — and I have patches of great determination, only to weaken and give up under all the other pressures of life. It would be easy to be overcome by the sense of guilt.

In fact guilt does not dominate my life; it never has entirely, for all the stabs of pain it may have occasioned. In purely human terms, life's pressures have prevented it taking over. I remember once going to see my doctor when I felt particularly drained and saying, 'I suppose I ought to give up my job. I'm just trying to cope with too much'. He wisely said that I should not; that it was very important, having a child like Arthur, to have something else to fill my mind. There are deeper reasons for the present absence of guilt which we will discuss later; but one important factor is that my relationship with Arthur has become much less self-centred and self-concerned. I am relaxed with him in a way I never used to be, however much I managed to give the impression I was.

I am sure that this is connected with the fact that I have become less possessive, more detached. This does not mean I love him the less. What it means is that the selfish element in my love has been purged away. It makes me realize how very self-centred love can be. When any of us worry about husband or child — perhaps they have not arrived home on time — we are not so much concerned about them, as about our own potential loss. When I shared

Arthur's distress it was also my distress, and we mutually fed each other's distress to the mutual benefit of neither. Sympathy (suffering with) can be a destructive and self-centred thing, a kind of proving that we really care. It is only when we can let go, become detached that we really love the other person for himself, allowing him to be himself and do his own thing without the binding cords of possessiveness. And that is when the relationship, paradoxically, deepens. The sheer delight I now have in Arthur is balanced by an ability to shrug off his occasional desire to thrust me away and be left alone; by an ability to get irritated with his occasional refusal to co-operate and to act out the irritation, defusing the tension; by a genuine appreciation of his absence for a few days once a month instead of the agony it once was to let him go. And I am sure that I am less of an ogre to him — not that he has ever been totally negative in his attitude to me — far from it. It has always been clear that he responded to me more than to anyone else. But there have certainly been times when I guess it has been a bit of a love-hate relationship. His affection for my mother is much less ambiguous.

Until the last few months he saw relatively little of his Granny. She was living in Belfast and visits were not very frequent. However, when the children were small we often went to Northern Ireland both for Easter and for our summer holiday, and Granny always did sterling service in baby-minding while we got out for days' walking. The extraordinary thing is that even when quite small and very limited, Arthur always seemed to know her after months of not seeing her. He even seemed to recognize her at Birmingham airport once — totally out of any familiar context. Whenever she comes now he climbs on the sofa beside her (it used to be on her knee), and responds to her play, her singing, her tickling, with smiles, giggles and greater and greater excitement. He has even begun to demand her exclusive attention, turning her face towards him if she looks away. He now recognizes the drive to her bungalow down the road, and marches up to the door with enthusiasm, saying 'eh-oo Aa-er'. He has recently tried saying 'ung-ee', sometimes to her, sometimes to me, and we have a friendly rivalry as to whether it is Mummy or Granny he is trying to say. Probably it is both, but I often feel that she has the advantage of being like me but not having to do all the nasty things to him!

In the past his other grandmother was even more important in his life. Nanny lived with us. She was there when he came in from school, and every day he would crawl upstairs as soon as he came home and go straight into her room to watch the television. I have sometimes wondered what Arthur made of her death and the consequent changes. There were inevitably some tensions from having three generations in the house, but the compensations outweighed them. We simply could not have managed during the years with young children without the presence of Nanny, and for five years, Grandad too. It meant we could slip out on errands, have the occasional evening out together, rely on someone being in when the children returned from school. The extended family makes problems like Arthur containable, even for a career-minded mum. I began full-time work as a Lecturer at the University when Arthur was four and Edward two: immediately my relationship with the children improved. Nothing is more destructive than an unfulfilled mother tied to young children all hours of the day — not that that was ever quite my situation. There was always a bit of research ticking away. We had nursery arrangements for the children once I was working full-time; but even so the presence of Nanny was invaluable.

And so was the reassurance of all our parents when our

Arthur problem became known. Nanny had been through
the same kind of thing with her second child, who had been
even more limited than Arthur. I still remember Grandad
saying, 'He's going to be all right', as Arthur began to crawl.
They all shared and supported. Arthur's great-grandmother
at over ninety spent hours lying on the floor with him
teaching him to clap his hands, and left all her savings for
his future when she died. My father and my uncle have
willingly taken their turn at 'Arthur-sitting'. We knew all
along that the wider family mattered. We certainly have
proved it.

Needless to say, the rock underlying all the shifting sands
of my feelings has been the care and support of Bob, my
husband. Temperamentally he is rock-like anyway, and his
experience of having a handicapped brother somehow
seemed to prepare him. From the very beginning he accepted it as just one of those things that happen, and we had
been unlucky. He has shared all the heat and burden of the
day in terms of caring and handling, feeding and changing,
more or less making Arthur his own when I had each new
baby to cope with. He has borne with me and borne with
Arthur through our emotional upsets. He shared my sense
that medical advance has been ambiguous, and that society
imposes an unnatural morality; he shared the burden of
hopelessness about the future. Even now it is hard to
foresee a real future for Arthur. But now we are both more
ready to let the future take its course and concentrate on
the present. We are through the wood; and it is in large
measure due to his steadfastness through all our difficulties, and his wretched sense of humour!

And what of William our youngest? He has always seemed
a special bonus. We intended to have only two children, but
in the light of Arthur's condition and the advice we were
given to have a predominantly normal family, we decided

49

to have a third. Arthur has been part of his life from the word go. There has never been embarrassment or jealousy. He responds with the utmost naturalness to the situation, and carries this over to an entirely natural response to other handicapped people. If all the world could grow up with this beautiful acceptance of people who seem odd or different, there would be no prejudice and no apartheid. Neither of the boys has had any qualms about bringing friends to the house; though perhaps puberty will introduce a shyness not apparent so far. What struggle there is in the family arises from the natural rivalry of normal, self-assertive, growing lads. Arthur is a focus of care and affection. He has been the catalyst of significant discoveries about human relationships. He has helped us all to a greater maturity.

In 1989 things are much the same for us all, though I know now that there is always a risk of return to distress, that I am still vulnerable and easily threatened by events or questions that trigger the old feelings. There has been no easy triumph, but the pain is shot through with joy, and the joy is pierced with pain.

Chapter 3

HOW CAN FAITH SURVIVE?

I thought I had accepted it. But at a deeper level I had not. I simply could not understand it. It was not just Arthur. He focussed my perception of the much bigger problem. If this world was created by the loving purposes of God, how could this sort of thing happen? If God intended people to grow to maturity in faith and love, what about those who were incapable of doing so? When we were first in Birmingham, Chris Hughes Smith, then minister of my church, came to visit, and some of this questioning came out. 'Can't you do it by taking seriously the I-Thou relationship?' he said. He was referring to the great Jewish theologian, Martin Buber[5], who had made much of the difference between the way we relate to a thing, an 'It', and the way we relate to a person, a 'Thou'. I felt I had no difficulty with understanding my relationship with Arthur as an 'I-Thou' relationship, but I found it difficult to cope with all cases in those terms. I now knew that there were cases far worse than his, indeed that there was such a thing as autism, a handicapped condition in which the person finds it impossible to relate to the external world or to other people. Re-reading Buber some years later, I began to see better what Chris was getting at. For Buber speaks of seeing even a tree as a 'Thou' and making a personal encounter with it; whether or not this is mystical is a nice question, but at least it opens up the possibility of personal relationship even with one who seems a non-person, and now I would be more ready to see that as a possibility, no matter how extreme the handicap.

[5] Martin Buber, *I and Thou*, English translation Walter Kaufman, T&T Clark 1970.

But then I could not see it. It was one thing to accept Arthur; it was another to come to terms with the great iceberg of suffering and tragedy hidden below him, as it were. This seemed to resist all attempts at justification. The problem of believing in a good God in the face of the tragedy and evil of the world was posed in a sharper way than ever before.

Under the surface the wrestling with this issue went on for years, and now and again the questions would become pressing, urgent, agonizing. They would contribute to the distress. When I was expecting my second child, I did not consciously worry. We had been assured that there was no genetic reason for Arthur's condition and the chances of having another handicapped child were hardly greater than with any other pregnancy. I remember, however, a well-meaning helper at the Birmingham Society's play-group saying, 'There's no need to worry. God won't let it happen again.' I did not say what I was thinking, but everything in me cried, 'If he let it happen once, why shouldn't it happen again? What about people who are carriers of a genetic defect and have one handicapped child after another?' I was not worried for myself. Indeed, I was surprisingly confident. But I could not accept a statement that seemed such a naive running away from reality. The questions were there and not easily solvable.

And in spite of that confidence of mine, which was real throughout my second pregnancy, there must have been underlying unacknowledged fear. I had been very angry about the way we were kept in the dark about Arthur's condition, and as I lay in the labour ward I decided that I must ask the Sister to make sure I was informed of anything wrong with my next baby immediately it was born. It was, I thought, a perfectly rational and reasonable request. I called the Sister. I began to explain, and completely broke down. That second labour was three hours longer than the first, and in the end I did not have the strength to deliver the baby myself. He was delivered with forceps. It is true that whereas Arthur had an abnormally small head, this well-developed child had an extra large one — all brain, in fact! So there were physical factors. But I suspect there may well have been unsuspected psychological ones too. I was carrying a good deal of suppressed anxiety. The fundamental questions had received no satisfactory answer, and those deeper uncertainties undermined what confidence I had.

Many years later I belonged to a group which met for fellowship and discussion. We began to tell each other our spiritual autobiographies. By then I thought I was finding my way back to a more confident faith, but I began by confessing that every now and again things happened which revealed that I still had not resolved my deepest questioning. A few weeks before, I had been to Arthur's school for a routine medical check-up. Almost out of the blue I had found myself reduced to tears. Outwardly I seemed to be coping with a very full life; inwardly there was still this huge blank. When I had finished my long confession, one member of the group commented that it sounded like a tragedy, and yet what a rich life I had had. It still felt like a tragedy, a living with meaninglessness. Sharing with that group was a kind of catalyst. For years I had struggled with the questions in utter loneliness. It made me confess things I had never shared with others before. The tragedy was not so much Arthur as my sense of abandonment, my inability to accept the existence and love of God at those deeper levels where it makes a real difference to one's life. I could still make a Christian confession; I still preached from time to time, and often found that Wesley's advice 'Preach faith till you've got it' came true — that it was when I was giving to others — and only then — that I had any real grasp on what I had to give.

A close friend speaks of discerning an underlying faith-fulness all through those years. But my experience was of an internal blank where God should have been. I had no hope for the future. Despair was lodged deep down inside, even if for the most part I got on with life and joked and played with the kids, and lectured in theology, and researched and wrote, passed for a Christian and went to church. Occasion-ally I would wrestle with meaningless prayer to a blank wall. It felt like a tragedy, yet my friend's comment on the richness of my life, came across as a healthy rebuke. It is since that evening that I have been enabled to climb out of my black hole and find complete release from the doubts and guilts and fears and self-concern that had imprisoned me.

It is important to recognize the links between doubt and the underlying emotional stress. There is a sense in which each fed the other, and neither could be resolved without the other finding its solution. But it is important to recog-nize also that the element of doubt was not simply a matter of self-concern. The personal distress was the catalyst for a far deeper challenge than I had faced before to the truth of Christian claims about the world, about the nature of God and his relationship with it. Not that I had not already faced the intellectual challenges posed by science, philosophy, history and so on. No one can read for a theology degree and not be faced with that kind of intellectual challenge. Nor is it a bad thing that that should be so. Christian faith is not blind faith. It is an attempt at a coherent view of life in all its aspects. If life does not measure up to that view, then that view will have to be modified or even rejected. It cannot represent the truth. I am not suggesting that the truth of Christianity can be proved by rational means. That is evidently not the case. But we have a responsibility to take seriously the facts and arguments which might falsify our beliefs. Furthermore the critical process helps us to see what the really essential things are, and what are secondary and peripheral matters. It drives us to probe beneath simple 'Sunday school' statements of belief to a deeper awareness of the truths of the Christian faith and their implications. Criticism is often feared as destructive by church people, but it is important that it should be embraced and valued for the positive benefits it can bring. Whether we are discussing biblical texts, or credal statements, or the nature of God, or anything else, it is necessary to refine our ideas and test out what we mean. If we have to abandon some over-simple conceptions in the process, so much the better. It does not necessarily mean we have abandoned Christian belief. We may even have rediscovered essential insights once central to the faith and now submerged by subsequent developments.

One of the most telling arguments against Christian belief in a loving Creator is the problem of evil. I had been all through the objections and the standard answers in my study of the philosophy of religion. I had decided that the arguments were not in the end entirely damaging and that I could go on believing in God. One of the books which had helped me to reach this conclusion was John Hick's *Evil and the God of Love*[6]. This is a brilliantly clear exposition of one helpful answer. The fundamental case, as I recall it, is that the development of moral beings, the process of 'soul-making' requires freedom and the right kind of world in which to exercise that freedom. Human beings were created with the potential for good or evil. The idea that Adam or humanity was once perfect and then fell into sin from that state of perfection is less convincing than the idea, to be found in early Christian tradition though largely later

[6]   John Hick, *Evil and the God of Love*, Macmillan 1966, Fontana 1968.

submerged, that Adam was somewhat like a child, imma-
ture, with potential for development, potential perfection
rather than actual perfection. Maturity comes to each
person as they struggle against suffering and evil. Penalties
for mistakes were bound to be built into the physical order
— in fact pain is a protection, a warning sign. Similarly
moral qualities, like love and courage, depend upon risk
and need for care and sympathy. God's purpose is this on-
going process of soul-making, and this was the best possible
world for that process to take place.

Now it is true that I had also heard a series of lectures by
Professor MacKinnon on the problem of evil, in which he
had forced us to contemplate the horror of evil and not be
satisfied with slick answers. There is a long history in
Christian philosophy of suggesting that evil is simply the
absence of good; Professor MacKinnon convincingly showed
that such a view simply could not cope with the phenomenon of malignant evil, positive active evil, sadism. I remember asking him once whether he was arguing for an ultimate
dualism, that is, the view that there is a power of evil at work
in the world, permanently warring against the power of
good. He intimated that he thought the possibility should
be taken very seriously.

Of course, such a possibility has something of a history in
Christian thought, though never as an ultimate dualism, an
eternal conflict. God, in the Judaeo-Christian tradition has
always been the originator of things and the ultimate victor,
even if there be a devil upsetting his works for the time
being. Lucifer was always depicted as a rebellious angel (his
name means 'Bearer of Light'), who fell from heaven. Hell
was God's punishment for him and his associates, who
having rebelled against God, now spent all efforts tempting
human beings to do wrong and so join them in torment.
Such a myth certainly helps to explain some of the evils over

which we have no control, but it does not resolve the problem of evil altogether. There is still the question why did God create Lucifer, or why did he let him fall? The Tempter may provide some explanation of human sin, but only by starting an infinite regress — who tempted Lucifer? God is still ultimately responsible. The Bible insists that God is one and he shares his power with no one, that God is the Creator. In places the Bible even suggests that disaster and suffering come from God — as his judgment. So whatever has gone wrong with the world, it must be God's responsibility. The horror of attributing some of the nastiest evils of this world to God makes the devil idea attractive, and there are some texts in the Bible which seem to suggest that the problems of the world are caused by a cosmic conflict between God and the powers of evil. The difficulty of apportioning blame for that malignant evil which seems to take possession of individuals and societies, even societies made up of decent, well-meaning people, makes the idea of demonic possession attractive. As Professor Mac-Kinnon hinted, dualism cannot be lightly dismissed. There does seem to be a struggle between good and evil that transcends the human scale. But I have never found the personification of evil as a demon god satisfactory or helpful, nor do I think it is the fundamental biblical view: even where Satan appears, he is often depicted as God's policeman or training officer, the one who sets tests of character, brings accusations in the heavenly court, etc., rather than being God's hostile opponent (e.g. the book of Job). The fundamental biblical view, and the one maintained in the Judaeo-Christian tradition, is that the only real ultimate is God. So whatever subsidiary beings you may posit, the problem is still God's responsibility.

Starting from this position, I had found John Hick's book reassuring. I was also prepared to accept the convenient distinction, again an idea with deep roots in Christian thinking, that there is a difference between physical evils and moral evil, that many of the things we think are evil are not really so but have a positive purpose. The only real evil is the result of human choice. In this way, God's responsibility is reduced. He is responsible only in so far as he allowed human beings freedom to choose.

Arthur challenged all these convenient assumptions and easy solutions. If God's purpose was 'soul-making', what about a new human being without the potential to respond and grow and mature in faith and in virtue? Even if I could allow that there was something good in my relationship with Arthur, that he was a trigger for deeper love, he represented the cases where there is no potential, the cases where handicap does not produce greater love but the kind of desperate burden that causes a marriage to crack, distorts the development of other children and leads to family breakdown. I began to see clearly the profound ambiguity of suffering and its power to discriminate, to bring out the best and bring out the worst in people. I could no longer accept the simple distinction between physical and moral evils because they seemed closely related to one another. The phenomenon of handicap can produce a naive sentimentality which refuses to admit it is an evil, but everything in me protested against it as cruel and unnecessary. And if, as I had always been led to believe, every individual is important to God, how could he afflict even one of his creatures in this way, let alone the two per cent of humanity that is born with some handicap or other, denying them the possibility of fullness of life? In terms of traditional Christian views about God's loving purposes I could make no sense of it.

Catholics have a long and impressive tradition of caring for the handicapped, and I remember hearing a nun say once, 'You can see the soul peeping out through their eyes.' She voiced that Catholic respect for the spiritual element in everyone, the Catholic perception of Christ in even the most afflicted, disadvantaged and outcast from human society. It is a noble tradition, and I would now feel there is much to learn from it. But at the time when I heard the remark, it helped me not one whit. It was expressed in terms of that long-standing view of a person as a being composed of soul and body, the body being the vehicle of the real individual. I had learned through my theological studies that this is not a biblical view, but had come into Christianity from Platonism. I knew that philosophically such an understanding had come into severe difficulties in this century. The 'ghost in the machine' notion of a human being simply could not work. There was nowhere to 'locate' the soul. The brain is a physical organ with a physical connection to the body through the nervous system. It is impossible to imagine a disembodied person because our physical selves are part of our total personality. We are a psychosomatic whole — that long word simply expresses the integral unity of our selves as physical, emotional, psychological, intellectual selves. We cannot be 'divided' into soul and body. I was even more convinced of this by the experience of Arthur. A damaged brain means that the whole personality is damaged and lacks potential for development. It depends to some extent on which part of the brain is damaged, of course. Some spastics have a very high IQ trapped in a body over which they have so little control they cannot speak or do anything for themselves. In those cases there clearly is some ground for speaking of a 'soul' or 'mind' peeping out through their eyes. But brain-damaged children may have normally functioning bodies, and yet be incapable of making sense of the world, responding to it or communicating with it (as in the case of autism). There will be no eye-contact, no response. In what sense do such people have a soul? Many will have physical handicaps consequent upon an inadequately functioning brain, like Arthur who had the potential physical capability for walking but never learned to do so. Such persons often seem to exist in a world of their own, to be quite vacant and unresponsive, eyes dull and uncomprehending, unable to interpret the sense-impressions they get from seeing or hearing. For years Arthur did not turn to look when he heard a noise behind him, not because there was anything wrong with his physical capacity to hear, but because he had not developed the understanding to react. It is quite unrealistic, it seems to me, to talk of a 'soul' peeping out through their eyes.

The biblical view of a human person is not consistent with that kind of understanding anyway. According to the Old Testament, God made a clay figure and breathed his life into it. That is a story expressing the dependence of a living human being upon the Spirit of God. Death is the absence of God, and in the Old Testament what remained of a person after death was simply a shade of his former self in the grave or the underworld, apart from the life of God. When ideas about life after death began to develop, what prophets foresaw was the re-creation of a human being by the resurrecting of his body from the grave and the gift of God's life, a restoration of the whole creature, a psychosomatic whole. It was later Christianity that re-interpreted this in terms of immortality of the soul.

Now if this thinking is right, then the easy option of thinking that a soul survives whatever the state of body or brain, and that all the wrongs of this world will be put right in the next, simply will not do in the case of handicapped people. We must, of course, recognize that physically handicapped people are people in their own right with the capacity to make their own decisions, organize their own lives, and so on. Many of the mentally handicapped have much more potential in this kind of area than used to be thought. The development of the full potential of even the most limited is clearly important. But there are people, like Arthur and more limited than Arthur, of whom it is very difficult to speak of some kind of 'person', distinct from the brain-damaged body, which might or might not survive death. To justify their condition in terms of the soul peeping out through the eyes which will be refined by the afflictions of this world and suddenly come to some sort of flowering in the life to come, is entirely implausible. The normal development of personality or mind or 'soul' is just so hampered. I once heard a graduate student attempting in a seminar to rescue the idea of a 'soul' from the battering it has received by modern philosophy, and in the ensuing discussion I found myself stressing, with a good deal of emotion, the case of brain-damaged persons as an objection. There is no 'ideal Arthur' somehow trapped in this damaged physical casing. He is a psychosomatic whole. Granted all the difficulties in asserting a doctrine of bodily resurrection, it does at least preserve that profound integration of our selves which is inescapably part of being what we are in this world and in our experience. It also implies the *reality of death*, and the dependence of all life upon God. There is no good reason for dreaming about automatic *post mortem* survival, either on philosophical grounds or on the basis of the Bible.

And this brings us on to another problem — healing. What sense would it make to hope for 'healing' in cases like this? Suppose that some faith-healer laid hands on Arthur tomorrow and all his damaged brain cells were miraculously healed, what then? Brains gradually develop over the years through learning. There are sixteen (now twenty-two)years of learning process that he has missed out on. In what sense could we expect normality, even if the physical problems were sorted out? The development of our selves as persons is bound up with this learning process. Of course it is all very complex; I am sure there are inbuilt genetic characteristics which affect this learning process and the development of personality — my other two sons have been different from one another in their personality and interests from the beginning. But what I am getting at is the fact that personality is not something distinct from the whole process of learning and maturing. Now Arthur has personality at his own limited level. He has a mind of his own which sometimes makes our lives a bit difficult. But I find it impossible to envisage what it would mean for him to be 'healed', because what personality there is is so much part of him *as he is*, with all his limitations. 'Healed' he would be a different person.

A number of years ago I was contacted by a woman with Pentecostal links who had a daughter with Down's Syndrome, though she seemed to flit from church to church in her search for a solution to her problem. She had had a vision of the Virgin Mary who appeared and told her the precise date on which her daughter was to be healed. The date came and went. She concluded she had not had enough faith, or had not carried out some task she had been told by the Lord to do. The whole saga was repeated time and time again. Some years after we had lost contact, I suddenly received yet another letter announcing the date of the miracle soon to be accomplished. At the time I was very worried about the woman's state of psychological health. It seemed to me that this was another manifestation of the 'I will do anything' syndrome referred to earlier, and that it was evidence of the fact that she had never really accepted her daughter. She maintained that she accepted her daughter but did not accept her condition. The reason

I mention this now is because it is linked with what I have just been saying. She was behaving as if her daughter's condition was some kind of sickness which could simply be removed. But research has shown that Down's Syndrome is caused by a mutation in the genetic inheritance of the person. Every cell in the body is affected by this. The whole person is as she is because the basic make-up of this person is as it is. What sense does it make to speak of healing? It would be a different person who would appear. It would be a bit of magic out of a fairy story.

My dealings with this woman were profoundly disturbing. I did my best to help her pastorally, standing alongside her, sharing my own problem, and trying to help her to accept her daughter in a positive way. I was disturbed at two levels. One was to do with her understanding of faith. It seemed to me that she had turned faith into a kind of 'work' and was trying to screw herself up to enough of it to make the miracle happen. I did not think that that was what the Bible meant by faith. St Paul was trying to get people to see that it was not their own efforts which brought about salvation, but the sheer grace and love of God. Faith is accepting what God has done, and trusting him for all that is to come. Faith is not desperately trying to believe six impossible things before breakfast.

Yet my own state of doubt and uncertainty made it difficult to affirm the trust and hope involved in that kind of faith. Part of me was as desperate as she was for a miracle, and our contacts made me aware of my own desperate desire to be let off the hook. I thought I had accepted Arthur; but I too had not accepted the situation fully. I could not make sense of it. Nor could I pray for a miracle with my mind convinced of its possibility. There was that desperate cry of the heart, but no faith that such a prayer could be answered. I did not think her understanding of faith was right or indeed biblical; but I had little confidence in my own faith, either.

Years later I preached on perseverance to a black congregation belonging to one of the African independent churches. I spoke of Arthur. By then I had found a more confident faith. But again I found myself disturbed when they pressed the question afterwards — had I prayed for healing? I said 'yes'; but in my heart of hearts I knew that I had never prayed with conviction. For all the reasons given above, I could not see that healing was conceivable. Not that I would now dismiss out of hand cases of apparently miraculous cures for a considerable range of conditions. Our bodies are clearly not quite the machines presupposed by some scientific medicine. We are psychosomatic wholes, and psychological factors like morale, and faith, clearly contribute to our total health. I believe the healing ministry of the church has an important place alongside orthodox medicine, and that unexpected and apparently mysterious healings can and do take place. But it is still difficult for me to extend that to mental handicap. Most of the cells in our bodies have recuperative properties, and healing is a stimulation of those healing properties into action. Brain cells have no such recuperative properties. Stroke victims lose certain brain cells for ever; they may learn to compensate by stimulating other cells to take over the functions of the lost cells, but the damaged part of the brain is never restored. There is nothing that can be done about damaged brain cells. For this reason, as well as for the reasons concerned with learning and maturing given earlier, I simply find cures for mental handicap, miraculous or otherwise, incredible. I have no doubt it is possible to maximize potential, to stimulate other cells to take over lost functions, and so on. But cure in the sense of the restoration of normality I cannot comprehend, let alone hope for. These were the reasons I had never been able to pray for Arthur's healing with any conviction. To arouse hopes of miraculous healing seemed to me to be dangerous and cruel, delaying the effective acceptance of the situation in a positive way.

Yet there was this niggling feeling — suppose I just lacked faith. Could I actually limit the possibilities if God really was God? Not so long ago I shared this question with the fellowship group to which I have already referred. It just came up naturally during the course of our discussions one evening. I told of how, when challenged on whether I had prayed for Arthur's healing, I had said 'yes', because it was true that there had been times when I had cried out for it in desperation with every cell of my being, but I knew deep down I had never prayed with any conviction. I outlined my sense that God had not created a fairyland in which impossible things could happen by waving the magic wand of faith. If God created this world he is responsible for the way it is. Salvation cannot be discontinuous with creation. Extraordinary things happen maybe. Things maybe happen which we cannot explain. But the definition of miracles as a breaking of the laws of nature has always seemed to me to be theologically suspect. God surely works with the processes that he built into the created order, not against them.

It is not a question of whether God *can* do miracles, but whether he *does*. If he does, then a capricious element is introduced which is neither consistent with his faithfulness nor our experience. He has set us in a world where accidents happen, and we have to bear the consequences, whether they are the result of blameworthy carelessness or just one of those things. How could I pray with conviction for Arthur to be healed? It did not fit with my understanding of God or the world. And yet, was it just a failure of faith? A member of the group put the whole thing into perspective by saying quite simply, 'Does anyone expect a severed limb to be restored by faith healing?' Brain damage is injury of that kind; it is genuine loss, real death or absence of vital brain cells. Whatever we may believe about our ultimate destiny, we all accept certain limitations as part of the structure of this life — and one of those is the irreversibility of death. We do not expect even the greatest saint to rise again to *this* life, whatever we make of the resurrection of Jesus. The healing of a damaged brain is simply implausible.

Despite all this, I find myself still in 1989 capable of reacting to questioning about prayer for healing in a way that reveals my insecurity: it is a deeply threatening question. And when I am encouraged to be honest about my 'wanting' before God, there's a level of distress and pleading that gainsays my inability to pray for what I want. I can and have prayed for Arthur's life not to be prolonged: but both prayer for miracle and prayer for death is prayer for let-out. Mind and heart are sometimes deeply at variance. But God is a God 'unto whom all hearts are open, all desires known', and I can only let it all rest in his hands. 'Do not look forward to what might happen tomorrow,' said St Francis de Sales: 'the same everlasting Father who cares for you today, will take care of you tomorrow, and every day. Either he will shield you from suffering, or He will give you unfailing strength to bear it. Be at peace then and put aside all anxious thoughts and imaginations.'

All the struggle with doubts and questions described in this chapter just shows how ambiguous a religious view of life can be. If you take a purely naturalistic view of the world, as my scientist husband does, it is so much easier. Accidents happen and you just have to make the best of it. Acceptance of the situation, courage in coping with it, getting the maximum human value out of it is all that matters. From the time I met Bob I had been jogged out of the complacency that afflicts Christian groups as they discuss what difference Christianity makes to people's lives. It is not true that Christians are better people. My husband is one of the best people I know. Nor is it true that faith gives you the edge in coping with the problems of life. It may delude you into never facing reality, into false hopes, into a sentimental and unrealistic optimism about things. Or it may compound your problems by setting up a sharp dichotomy between an accepted idea of what the world is like and the awful reality you actually have to face. My experience has proved that religion is no escapism. It led me into deeper and deeper agonies over the state of the world. It raised questions and difficulties which the non-believer never had to face. For many years I felt it would be so much easier just to give up on this Christian nonsense, the absurdity of claiming that this rotten world was created by a good loving God, the illusion that with enough faith and goodwill everything will somehow be put right and the kingdom of God arrive. But somehow I could not live with that way out. There was something in me that resisted it as an easy option; there was an imperative in me to find again the world of meaning which had once energised my life, to find that there was not a blank wall or a black hole, but God. I lived with a dreadful sense of loss. My doubts sapped my energy, deepened my distress, my sense of tragedy, my hopelessness. I was deeply depressed by the experience of living in a God-less world. Yet I could not just drift into a fantasy world and pretend that everything was all right after all. The challenges were inescapable. I had to go on wrestling, fighting in the dark.

It is surprising how sometimes a biblical story seems to express one's experience. Only recently someone compared my experience with the story of Jacob wrestling with a man at the Jabbok ford. Jacob would not let the man go,

67

Chapter 4

IS GOD THERE?

The place where he wrestled with God, Jacob called Penuel, which means 'face of God'. He said, according to the story, 'I have seen God face to face'. I am not sure I can imagine what it would be like to see God face to face, and in any case elsewhere in the Old Testament it is said that no one can see God and live; but I understand how one can speak of coming face to face with reality, and in that kind of sense I do not think the title of this chapter inappropriate to my experience.

From the perspective of the present it is tempting to look back and see everything in terms of 'before' and 'after'. But it would be very misleading to present my progress quite like that. There are important continuities in my understanding, and the present is the fruit of many ups and downs. It was not a case simply of dark years of doubt in which life was permanently overcast, and a sudden clearing of the skies. It was a period of storms, with shafts of light piercing the clouds, and then the sky becoming overcast again; followed by a period of blue sky occasionally interrupted by cloudy patches. Besides, it is important to bear in mind that everyday life went on pretty normally for year after year, with the typical tensions and joys, laughter and teasing and irritation of family life, accompanied by the frustrations and successes of a developing career in teaching and research. No one could have lived with me if I had been in a constant state of anxiety over the doubts and questions outlined in the last chapter. They were simply an underlying, unresolved agenda which from time to time surfaced and preoccupied my mind, even as I coped with

69

the everyday pressures of life.

The problem of God's reality was not first posed by the crisis of Arthur. I had become aware through studying philosophy of religion that there were no satisfactory arguments for the existence of God: the whole thing just works out about 50-50, and people make up their minds on quite other grounds. I had been profoundly challenged by meeting and marrying someone who did not share the beliefs with which I had grown up and by which I had come to live. Strangely enough it was that experience which gave me an unconventional 'argument' for God's existence. The extraordinary happiness of marriage had so filled me with gratitude and the sense that something had happened to me which I in no way deserved, that I felt there had to be someone to say thank you to. I still think that was a profound discovery, and I am sure that the core of Christian devotion is wonder at the grace of God and thanksgiving for our creation, preservation and all the blessings of this life. However, I recognized that it was no theoretical answer to the problem of God's reality. It was demonstrably possible for people to live very good and effective lives without worrying about God at all. So the possibility that religion was all illusion had to be taken seriously. I doubt if many religious people actually sense the presence of God all the time. I certainly did not.

The immediate shock of knowing Arthur's condition was a bit like a bereavement, in more ways than one. I have noticed several times that God seems more real than at any other time in the face of death, particularly the death of close relatives. Similarly my distress had within it a strangely transcendent assurance which lasted for some time. I somehow knew that I was borne up not only by the love and support of my husband, but also by the love of God. Years later I came across this rather soppy little poem:

A meeting was held quite far from earth.
'It's time again for another birth',
Said the Angels to the Lord above,
'This Special Child will need much love.
His progress may seem very slow,
Accomplishments he will not know,
And he'll require extra care
From the folks he meets down there.
He may be slow to run or play,
His thoughts may seem quite far away.
In many ways he won't adapt
And he'll be known as handicapped.
So let's be careful where he's sent.
We want his life to be content.
Please Lord, find the parents who
Will do a special job for You.
They will not realise right away
The leading role they're asked to play.
But with this child sent from above
Comes stronger faith and richer love.
And soon they'll know the privilege given
In caring for the gift from heaven.
Their precious charge, so meek and mild,
Is heaven's Very Special Child.'[8]

It expresses very much how I felt as I made the initial adjustments and faced the facts about Arthur. There was a shaft of light before the gathering storm-clouds. I remember talking to the minister in Cambridge before we left, and saying that I felt I should do more preaching after we moved. Soon after we moved, however, there occurred that conversation referred to earlier with Chris, my new minister. The doubts were beginning to be expressed. His reference to Buber's 'I-Thou' relationship must have meant something to me or I would not have remembered it so vividly — we went for a walk together pushing Arthur in the

[8] An anonymous poem taken from the anthology, *Answer me World*, ed. Christine Zwart and Peter Pascoe, NSMHC 1975, p. 30.

pram through the local park, and it was there he made the suggestion. It did help me with my own problem, I guess; but the bigger difficulty of those who were incapable of any kind of relationship still troubled my mind. The whole hopeless mess the world was in and the impossibility of doing anything about so many of the problems seemed to loom larger and larger, focussed by the helpless baby we were pushing along. How could any sense be made of it all? How could I go on believing in God? It must have been some years later that I asked Chris if he could take account of Mental Handicap week in the service on the relevant Sunday. He turned the tables on me and asked me to preach. I could hardly refuse. Yet what did I have to say? My questions were still unresolved. How could I preach on that subject of all subjects? In fact he did me a good turn, though I had some desperate days wondering what on earth to do. It was under that pressure that I had the beginnings of a solution given to me.

I found myself struggling with the story of the man blind from birth told in John's Gospel, chapter 9:

> His disciples asked him, 'Rabbi, who sinned, this man or his parents, that he was born blind?' Jesus answered, 'It was not that this man sinned, or his parents . . .'

Commentators usually point out that this is criticism of the Old Testament idea that sin brought judgment and suffering, therefore suffering must imply sin. What they do not always realize is that the criticism still needs to be made. I was horrified once when a helper with the Birmingham Society reported to me that she had been travelling on a hired minibus, picking up handicapped children around the city, and the driver had said to her, 'What on earth have the parents done to have children like these?' I say I was horrified, and yet there must be something instinctive about that idea. As already noted, it is said that the parents of handicapped children often feel guilty, and I had myself momentarily faced the possibility that Arthur was God's punishment for something I had done — and rapidly dismissed the idea. That kind of God I certainly could not believe in.

That kind of explanation, then, I found dismissed by Jesus, but what other explanation was offered?

> It was not that this man sinned or his parents, but that the works of God might be manifest in him.

What an appalling statement! Could it really be suggested that that man and his family had to put up with all those years of suffering and handicap just so that Jesus could wave a magic wand and heal him to demonstrate his power? I found myself protesting with all the protest that had been generated by Arthur. That simply did not fit, to my mind, with the picture of Jesus' compassion found in the other Gospels, or with any acceptable idea of God. And then it began to dawn on me. Not for nothing had I studied John's Gospel and read it in Greek with students. It is well known that this story is placed in the Gospel as a 'sign' demonstrating the saying 'I am the light of the world'. It is intended to be read as an acted parable. As Jesus gives light to the blind man, so he brings light to the world. But the Prologue to the Gospel has already hinted that when the light shone in the darkness, the darkness could not grasp it, and here we find the next sentences pointing ominously forward to the cross:

> We must work the works of him who sent me while it is day; night comes, when no one can work.

Jesus the light of the world is to be snuffed out, because the darkness could not grasp the light. And yet everything in

73

this Gospel points to the cross as the hour of glory. In the end Jesus did not waft away the darkness of the world, all its sin and suffering and hurt and evil, with a magic wand. He entered right into it, took it upon himself, bore it, and in the process turned it into glory, transformed it. It is that transformation which the healing of the blind man fore-shadows.

Seeing this story and indeed the whole drama of John's Gospel in these terms, gave me the clue, and the sermon. There could not be any philosophical answer to the prob-lem of evil; not one is fully satisfactory. The only answer, the only thing that makes it possible to believe in God at all, is the cross. In fact I would now want to acknowledge that some of the traditional answers have a certain wisdom, and do provide partial solutions, aids to understanding. But I would still maintain that a properly Christian response to the problem of evil has to begin with the cross, with an understanding of atonement. We do not begin by explain-ing evil away, justifying God, excusing him for the mess he has made of his creation. We begin by contemplating the story which tells of God taking responsibility for the evil in his world, by entering it himself, taking it upon himself, in all its horror, cruelty and pain.

It must have been round about this time that I wrote a little book called *Sacrifice and the Death of Christ*.[9] In general I would not think it a good thing for people to work through their own hang-ups in the guise of academic research, though research does need to be fuelled by passionate interest and commitment to a subject. In that book, the research I had done for my thesis before Arthur was born, came together with some of the insights I was beginning to develop as a result of my experience. The thesis had been

[9] Frances Young, *Sacrifice and the Death of Christ*, SPCK 1975, reissued SCM Press 1983.

concerned with the way the early Christians took over the language of sacrifice from the Old Testament and other religions of the time, and used it to express their commitment, their worship, and above all the death of Christ. It therefore dealt in particular with the way Christians understood the cross as atoning in the first four centuries of Christian thought. As a more popular presentation of my conclusions evolved out of a series of Lent lectures I had given in central Birmingham, the publishers encouraged me to try and develop the discussion of how all this might be relevant to Christian belief today. I was hesitant — to a scholar the whole thing seemed too speculative, not sufficiently tied to concrete material which was there to be interpreted. But again someone was doing me a good turn, coaxing me into a greater confidence in thinking things through and drawing upon modern literature and drama and experience to 'translate' insights of the past into terms comprehensible in a quite different culture. When it was done I realized that even though he never appears in the text, Arthur had in fact made a tremendous contribution to the final section of the book. It was dedicated cryptically to A.T. I could not then bring myself to explain the reference, though those who knew me must have seen through it. When the book was reprinted in 1983, I was able to acknowledge in a new preface that writing the book had been a significant stage in my pilgrimage towards understanding. The way back from doubt was through the cross and the atonement, through the Bible and Christian doctrine, through preaching, lecturing, studying and writing. There were long periods when the heat of all this activity, and the positive gains made in understanding kept the darker side of things at bay.

In fact work was a good therapy in more ways than one. Sometimes it was only afterwards that I would begin to discern the significant relationship between things I had been working on and my own problems with faith. It was at a quite late stage in the process that I recognized the extent to which my professional concern with the doctrine of Christ's humanity had a profound bearing upon the understanding of atonement towards which I was moving. If the presence of God within all the evil and suffering of humanity was the fundamental Christian insight, then the reality of Jesus' humanity was vital to the story. It was not this that had originally drawn me into involvement with the group that produced *The Myth of God Incarnate*,[10] but by the time we reached the discussions in *Incarnation and Myth*,[11] it had come to have over-riding importance. The initial concern was to be true to the contingencies of history, true to the logic of the biblical and doctrinal studies in which I was engaged. I had begun to feel that at the popular level mere lip-service was paid to the humanity of Jesus, and because believers did not take this important element of their faith seriously, most people thought that Christianity was about some semi-divine supernatural being popping down to earth for a bit, acting like some superman (or perhaps like ET), and popping back up to heaven again. It was no wonder people dismissed it all as incredible. But a little awareness of the process by which the classical Christian dogmas and creeds came to be formulated is enough to show that most claims were confessions made for Jesus by his followers, and the popular picture is a mere caricature of Christian belief — indeed, it is virtually the same as one of the most bitterly fought heresies of the fourth century.

I was concerned for truth and for honesty. But I found that what I was affirming began to speak at a deeper level. Like us, Jesus had to live by faith, as the New Testament

[10] *The Myth of God Incarnate*, ed. John Hick, SCM Press 1977.
[11] Incarnation and Myth, ed. M. D. Goulder, SCM Press 1979.

clearly affirms, especially in the Epistle to the Hebrews.
Jesus did not have some abnormal faculty which gave him
some advantage over the rest of us. He was 'handed over'
(to use the term stressed in a recent book by W. H. Vanstone, whose writings I would strongly recommend[12]), made
vulnerable to the powers political and religious that wanted
to get rid of him, suffered dread and fear and desire to
escape, physical pain, intimidation and ridicule, torture
and death, and a sense of final abandonment, by supporters, friends, even God. This was no make-believe. He was
human, and he was subjected to some of the worst evil
human beings are capable of inflicting on one another, and
to the deepest darkness of the human spirit. To think that
he had some special knowledge or some unique advantage
over the rest of us is to undo the story. Jesus was a human
being. No doubt he had a very special sense of vocation; no
doubt he had a unique role to play. But exactly what he did
and said is a matter for careful historical research, not for
dogmatic statements made in advance of careful investiga-
tion.

My concerns as a professional scholar and historian were
not at variance with my concern for getting at the nub of
what Christian doctrine has sought to affirm; nor with my
developing understanding of the cross and atonement. At
the heart of it all is the cry reported by Mark's Gospel, 'My
God, my God, why hast thou forsaken me?' Jesus had
experienced even more acutely the abandonment and
desolation that I knew in my heart of hearts. It was only
because he had, that the other side of the story was significant: there in that utter absence of God, was the presence
of God. So the half and half picture of a supernatural semi-
divine being, already in fact rejected by the church when

[12] W. H. Vanstone, *The Stature of Waiting*, Darton, Longman and Todd 1982; see
also *Love's Endeavour, Love's Expense*, Darton, Longman and Todd 1977.

Arianism was excluded, is a totally inadequate understanding of the term 'Son of God'. For the story to mean anything for our salvation, it had to be about the real presence of God himself in a genuine human situation: fully God and fully man.

Ten years ago when I was involved in this work, I tried to understand the fully God and fully man formula in terms of two concurrent stories, as John Robinson had done, rejecting the idea that the philosophical talk of 'divine substance' and 'human substance' had much meaning. Since then, as a result of a more profound engagement with the material in the research for *From Nicaea to Chalcedon*,[13] I think I have come to understand metaphysics better, and to grasp some things about how the church fathers of the fifth century sought to explicate this paradox which I did not quite see then. If we talk about Christ being fully God and fully man we tend to get in a muddle because we assume it is rather like saying a liquid is fully water and fully wine at the same time, and we know that is impossible. It is either water or wine or watered down wine. In fact this kind of muddle also confused the fifth-century discussion, because they got hung up on the word 'nature', and found themselves arguing about the question whether there was one nature or two natures. Whichever formula you went for, you tended to imply the wrong thing — a mixture of the two, or two not really united. Such problems arise because of confusion between metaphysics and chemistry. What one has to realize is that to talk of God is not to talk of a being like other beings, alongside other beings or in competition with them, or potentially dilutable by them. Because of the nature of God — transcendent and immanent, personal yet not limited as all persons we know are, incomprehensible simply because he is both in and not in, like and not like the

[13] Frances Young, *From Nicaea to Chalcedon*, SCM Press 1983.

beings he has created — it is not in principle impossible for God to be really present in a truly human being, or in plain ordinary bread and wine. For the most part our experience of God is of partial presence or apparent absence, but in Jesus and the eucharist, we glimpse possibilities which are not elsewhere realized. We can hardly imagine what it means to speak of God suffering and dying, yet Christians affirm that the cross of Jesus is not just the story of a man being a martyr, but the story of God taking responsibility for all the evil and sin and suffering with which his creation is afflicted, by entering into it and going through it, so that by his presence, the situation may be transformed and re-creation begin to happen. Such a story requires not only the divinity of Christ but the genuine humanity of Jesus.

It is clear then that at this stage I already understood that what would make a difference to everything was a sense of God's presence. There were times when I could affirm this insight with great conviction. But my experience was largely an experience of God's absence, and because of this, although apparently I had some ground of faith, it was somewhat shaky when the bad times hit us, and the distress and despair got the upper hand. And it was an entirely cross-centred faith. There was little joy or hope in it. The cross confirmed the grim reality of this world. It meant that I could entertain the possibility that God was within that grim reality, alongside us, and so hang on to some measure of belief. It was by acceptance of the situation bearing it positively that it could be overcome, I thought. But it was not easy. And God did not often seem very real. Certainly I expected no solution, no miracle; and it was in the next few years we had to cope with the particular problems of that distressing 'middle period' already described. I hardly had the sort of confident, resilient faith to cope triumphantly with all that. And in spite of friends, colleagues, church

79

people, I faced these deeper traumas entirely alone. There was at that stage no one with whom I could share, partly because of my own inhibitions, partly because of the sheer practicalities of containing all the pressures of family and professional life. There just did not seem to be time to find fellowship, or to cultivate the kind of intimate relationship in which the depth of my pain and doubt could be shared with anyone else. When it came to problems with faith, my husband could not help; for all his patience, he could not be expected to understand.

I cannot now put a precise date upon the formation of the group which I have previously introduced as having had a considerable effect upon my emergence from those overcast years. I was approached after church one Sunday by David Clark, a Methodist minister who is on the staff of Westhill College: would I be interested in our getting a group together, composed of people from the university, Selly Oak colleges and the Queen's theological college, so that some people from these various institutions had a bit more contact and could share concerns? I liked the idea, though was acutely conscious of the practicalities of my situation at home. It was difficult to take on too many evening commitments, since I was out all day, and had young children. Then there were those nights I was out doing extramural teaching: I have always felt that that job of communicating with the public outside the university is of vital importance. However, we went ahead and organized it on the basis that the group would always meet in my house, and not have more than half a dozen meetings a year. Many of the original members have now moved away, but there is still a group meeting (not now in my house! — family circumstances constantly evolve) which is the direct descendant of the initial gathering. It has always been ecumenical in character, Methodists and Anglicans, and for some time now a Roman Catholic.

The group quickly evolved into a kind of theological forum, but not of the formal academic kind. It became a fellowship in which our deepest theological concerns and questions about life were shared. It took a couple of years or more, meeting so infrequently, for each member to give his or her own theological autobiography, and reveal the points at which each had been confronted with his or her own experience of alienation or questioning or discovery. I was certainly not the only one for whom this process was of profound importance. The telling, the sharing was as important if not more important, than the responses. We all faced things in ourselves which we had been unable to face, or unable to put into perspective, or unable to divulge to others for a variety of reasons. We did not pray together. Somehow it never seemed to be the natural and appropriate response. The present group is different: we now meet for prayer and meditation from which discussion arises. Each of the stages in the changing life of the group has had its own character. Perhaps it has been this ability not to predetermine what the group is or what it is for that has been its most creative feature.

On the occasion when I told all, I do not remember much that was said actually making much difference. But it was not long after I had shared with the group that I had an experience which can probably be regarded as the fundamental breakthrough. It was only momentary, and I find it very difficult to place in terms of time of day or context in the life of the family. But I know precisely what chair I was sitting in, and that I was sitting on the edge of the chair, about to go off and do something or other around the house. It was one of those 'thought-flashes' that seem to have no context: 'It doesn't make any difference to me whether you believe in my reality or not.'

I had a sense of being stunned, of being put in my place. It is difficult to see why, really. It is after all a theological commonplace, and I do not think that I had thought for a very long time that my intellect could solve the problems. It was all so very ordinary, too. Nothing dramatic happened. I got up and got on with whatever I was going to do. I have not, however, seriously doubted the reality of God since that moment. It has become one of those things whose significance has constantly expanded as further reflection has taken place. It has deepened into an understanding of how judgment is built into the biblical understanding of God's presence. It has developed into more systematic insights into how we come by knowledge of God. At that point I did not discover God. God confronted me. I was brought face to face with his reality. If there is a 'before' and 'after', that is the most significant moment. But it is not the whole story.

The other really significant event I can more or less date. It was late November, or perhaps just into December, 1979. I had been to Kingswinford, in the Black Country, to take an extramural class. The nucleus of the class was the Local Preachers of the Circuit, and it was held on Methodist premises, though being a university class it was open to anyone from the general public. It was during my second series with the class, and I was tracing with them the history of how the creeds came to be formed, and discussing the basic issues involved in debates about Christian doctrine. That evening we had had a good meeting, and I suppose I was therefore on a bit of a 'high'. I have always felt strongly about the need for real theological discussion and awareness in the church. Here it had happened; and included in the group were interested non-Christians. So often, I feel, people reject Christianity on the wrong grounds — they simply do not know what it is about and dismiss superficial impressions of it as no better than fairy stories. But here we had really been engaged with the issues.

At a particular set of traffic lights in Dudley, another 'thought-flash' hit me, this time very much in a specific context. 'You should get ordained.' Between there and my home I had the whole of my life laid before me, and it seemed as if this was what it had all been leading up to. I do not know how I drove home — I must have been on automatic pilot. I was filled with an overwhelming joy and excitement, a sense of profound fulfilment, of the integration of every aspect of my life. It has been tempting to think of it as a Damascus road experience — for Paul that was really a 'call' not a conversion; but I have always said this a bit tongue in cheek. After all I was not blinded or I would have landed in the ditch and there would be nothing further to tell. Besides I have long had a suspicion of dramatic emotional experiences. They could so easily be explained away psychologically. In the next few weeks I managed to suppress what had happened and tell myself it was all because I had just had my fortieth birthday. I remembered I had said to a friend on that day that whereas I had been very depressed on my thirtieth birthday, I now felt very exhilarated, because I felt I was at last tooled up to do some worthwhile theological writing and had put the problems of the past behind me. So I let it all simmer down. I let all the objections and difficulties have their weight — and there were plenty. It all seemed so unrealistic.

But it did not go away. By this time our youngest child was five, and on Christmas day we expected two lively boys to invade our bed with their stockings and the contents thereof. We just hoped it would not be too early! It did not happen at all. The two of them played together and we were left alone. Suddenly I realized that this was the moment to tell Bob what I had been thinking. To my utter amazement he

raised no objections and simply said, 'It seems the fulfilment of everything you do'. That was an incredibly wonderful Christmas. I was inwardly full of wonder and praise all
day. In fact, from that moment in Dudley I had been filled
with an inexplicable joy, a song in my heart, which was to
continue for months. It was a dramatic difference from the
inner gloom and hopelessness of the past. Whereas I had
been anxious about the future, now I suddenly felt that if
this was right, the future must work out somehow. What had
happened was such a surprise that anything could happen.

Not that it really came out of the blue. When I had been
a student twenty years previously, I would certainly have
offered myself as a candidate for the ministry if it had been
possible for a woman to do so. I had in any case gone on to
read theology after I had finished my initial classics degree,
having very little idea where it would lead, but convinced it
was the right thing to do. Then my life had taken an
unexpected course, through my marriage and the consequent decision to try and follow an academic career, like my
husband. Throughout all those years I had always had the
question niggling away — what *was* God's will? Was I doing
the right thing? How did one find out what was God's will?
Such uncertainties continued to oscillate around through
the years of doubt.

Now I had a vision. The vision came out of the circumstances in which I had received the call. Somehow my life's
work was to do with bridging the gap between the world of
academic theology and the church. I felt convinced that it
meant *both* that I seek ordination as a Methodist minister
and that I stay in my university teaching post.

This is not the place for a full account of how I shared this
vision with various people, talked it through with them,
oscillated between feeling sure of a vocation and being
overwhelmed by the difficulties and objections, until I

reached a deep and settled conviction that this was what I had to do. Perhaps I should slip in the comment that I am the more convinced it was right now because of the fruit it has borne, but the relevant thing here is to try and sort out what it all has to do with Arthur and the problems and doubts he had epitomized. One of the questions I was asked as I passed through the various committees on my way to acceptance as a candidate for ordination, concerned my domestic situation and Arthur in particular — not surprisingly. I was able to affirm that even though I could not predict what the situation would be when Arthur left school, I was convinced it would work out somehow. My fears about the future had disappeared completely in a new found trust, hope and serenity, an openness to new possibilities, a readiness to take risks and let the unexpected happen. I could not rule out the possibility that, even though I was sure I should remain in university teaching for the present, I might eventually be led into circuit ministry. The future was no longer a fearful prospect, but an open vista.

I also insisted that Arthur would be part of my ministry. What I consciously meant when I said that was that the experience of Arthur had marked me and changed me and given me things I would not have otherwise had; but as we shall see, my words were to be fulfilled in concrete ways which I could not then foresee. What was then most important was that I found myself able to give thanks, even for Arthur, and for the years of doubt and testing which made the new experience of trust and hope so precious and profound. It was no longer a case of simply accepting Arthur, but of rejoicing in Arthur.

In fact it was the sense of vocation which changed me. I was quite overwhelmed by the sense that God had loved me all along, and somehow everything in my life fell into place.

It seemed as though there had been a hidden purpose running through everything. At one point it suddenly struck me that my brother Richard, after whom I had nearly named Arthur, had been convinced of a call to the ministry. It seemed extraordinary that I should find myself fulfilling his vocation, especially since his death had been the occasion which led my other brother to take over his instrument, the cello, and he is now the principal cellist of a professional orchestra. Somehow between us we had fulfilled what the lost member of the family should have been. Yet this was not the outcome of conscious planning or intention. I could no longer shrug off the idea of providence, no matter how difficult it be to give any kind of account to how it might work. Above all I felt extraordinary exultation. It was sheer amazement that one who had so little deserved it had been brought through such a wilderness of desolation and loneliness, and had never in fact been left alone, but always loved and guided.

Of course one does not go on living on that level of intensity for ever, but the peculiar sensitivity of those months when I lived with a song in my heart, left me changed. The clouds of distress and doubt and hopelessness have barely ever returned; when they have they have been rapidly dispersed. A new mother rode the trials of those months with Arthur's legs in plaster, sat up all night with him when distressed, and took it all with a new and profound calm. Guilt is purged away. It is possible now to live with uncertainty about the future, because who can guess the extraordinary things that lie in the future anyway? And I began to experience a release of inhibitions, an overflow of love towards other people such as I had not felt before. The burden on the pilgrim's back had been untied and had rolled off.

How far this change was apparent to other people I am

not sure. I am well aware that there are real continuities in myself and in my thinking. Much of what I experienced I had already grasped — even preached about. It was as though things I had long known, I now knew in a new way. Even the exultation I had had glimmerings of in earlier shafts of light, and the black hole was, I think, pretty efficiently concealed. But the fact remains: I have now known the joy of release, and nothing can ever be as bad again. If I have since been shown more of the depth of sin in myself and my fellow human beings, I have been able to bear more, because I know now the reality and love of God. Indeed, the whole of life appears different. I remember hearing someone say once that when you become a Christian it is as though a black and white film suddenly changed into colour. I thought it sounded a bit sentimental at the time, but my own experience is of a transfiguring something like that which is often expressed in love poems. The ordinary world acquires an extraordinary dimension. Indeed it has been just like falling in love all over again. The strange thing is that even this thought was not entirely new for me: I remember years ago when Archbishop Antony Bloom was conducting a mission on campus, I was involved in a panel, and found myself speaking warmly about the psychological similarity between sexual love and love of God in response to a student's question. It is in fact this aspect of my awareness of God which has prevented me responding to feminist theology with any great enthusiasm or even much sympathy — I might even mischievously suggest that it is men who need a goddess-figure, not women at all! As far as I am concerned, on the one hand God transcends all anthropomorphic idols — he is a mystery, beyond the personal; on the other hand, I know him in a relationship to which the relationship with my husband is the closest analogy — that remarkable sense of trust and

which trusts for all that is to come. It seems to me that one cannot escape from the reality of this world's corruption, the reality of sin, the reality of death. The biblical message is not about utopia tomorrow. It is at least in part about a dreadful cataclysm of destruction — the coming of judgment, the end of the world epitomized in the cross. Yet the agony and travail of the world are the birth-pangs of a new world, a new creation anticipated in the new Adam, Christ, and those who become part of his body. There is a partial realization of this new regime wherever the presence of God is actualized, even in the midst of the sins and disasters that surround us. The kingdom of God presses itself upon us, with its demands for justice and peace and love, and its promises that the oppressed are those who are blessed. But it is not possible for us to force it in or bring it about by our own efforts. It involves the re-creation of this corrupted order, and only God can do that. We are asked to respond by allowing ourselves to get caught up in the workings of his Spirit, living fearlessly because we can trust God whatever. . . . There is no way we can do anything about Arthur's condition, but God is in the situation bringing to birth good out of evil; and who knows what that means ultimately? I do not believe even now that cure is possible. But I do know that we are in the hands of God, and nothing else matters.

I do not want to repeat here what I have written elsewhere. Perhaps I can bring out the point another way. It often happens that a parable strikes home more effectively than other ways of expression, and the years of reading stories to young children made their own important contribution to my accumulating insights. I keep going back, particularly, to a tale written by the poet Ted Hughes called 'How the bee became'[15]. A demon lives in the centre of the earth, and one day pops out and sees the creatures God is

[15] Ted Hughes, *How the Whale Became and Other Stories*, Penguin 1971.

making. He is jealous. He watches how God fashions a creature in clay and then breathes life into it. Down below he tries various experiments which do not succeed, and eventually grinds up precious jewels into powder and dampens the powder with his tears to make clay. He then beats out the shape on his anvil and produces a stunningly beautiful creature. But he cannot breathe life into it. He tricks God into doing it for him, and then down below plays with his new living toy. But the creature is very sad. It has God's life and needs freedom. It has the demon's tears in its veins. One day the demon takes it up to the light to compare his beautiful creature with God's. The creature takes its chance and escapes. It is still not happy, because the demon's tears are always in its veins. So it begins to gather all the sweetness it can, flitting from flower to flower until it overflows with sweetness — and that is what we call honey. The bee has to go on from flower to flower all the time seeking sweetness. The moment it stops the gloom of the demon's tears overtakes it. The smart of its angry sting is the tear of the demon. 'If he has to keep that sweet, it is no wonder that he drinks sweetness until he brims over.' I do not suppose that the demon is a good explanation of the presence of sadness or sin in the world, but the image of drinking up the sweetness expresses beautifully the Christian's experience of depending upon the joy of God in the midst of the world's sadness — the kingdom here, yet not here.

Can These Dry Bones Live? was also about the capacity of the Bible to come alive. That is another important thing that has happened to me during my pilgrimage. I am not one of those people who gets on very well with little snippets of the Bible each day; in any case the Bible is, if I may put it that way, my profession. But over and over again it is recollection of, or attention to some part of the Bible that has given me the examples and the clues which have made sense of life and my experience of it. The Psalms have become my prayer book. The combination of realism and hope in the prophets, Paul's conviction of vocation and struggle to work out some understanding of what was happening in his mission, and many other things have come alive for me in a way that makes 'academic study' of the Bible and devotional use of it totally inseparable.

The most obvious book of the Bible one might expect to speak to this situation is of course the book of Job. I had always found the book of Job baffling when it comes to providing any kind of answer to the problem it raises. When God appears at the end, he does not give any satisfactory explanation. He simply tells Job to contemplate how clever he the Creator is, and suggests that Job should pay his respects — exactly what one of the comforters had suggested long ago. Why on earth should Job comply? Why do Job's questions and protests cease?

Some time ago I was to take a class on Job. It was part of an Old Testament course for the Centre for Partnership between Black and White. Teaching the pastors of black-led churches has been a learning experience of great importance in its own right, but also because I was forced to rediscover the Old Testament which is not my own specialist field. As I prepared for the class I found an answer to the long standing puzzle. All through the dialogues with the comforters what really galls Job is God's absence. He is sure that if God were present his innocence would be vindicated. In heaven, he believes, is one who will vindicate him against the false charge that he must have sinned or he would not be suffering ('I know that my redeemer liveth'). What satisfies and at the same time humbles Job is simply the reality and presence of God. What God says is irrelevant. In God's presence the demand for explanation ceases. God is sufficient in himself to bring a perspective which transcends and transforms. That is more or less my experience. Face to face with God, the problems do not disappear but they do appear different.

When I came to take the class I was prodded into seeing something else. I had picked out the salient points in each speech and created an abbreviated form of the dialogue which we worked through together. I still remember vividly one of the pastors saying, 'Do you think Job was blaspheming?' I suggested that the answer was 'yes' and 'no'. There surely is no greater blasphemy than to try and hide our real feelings from God in a load of pious platitudes, the bland things we think we ought to pray. Total honesty before God is not blasphemy. Job's protest had its validity. So did the cry of desolation from the cross, which could easily be taken as a rebuke: 'My God, my God, why hast thou forsaken me?' Yet when in God's presence, the new perspective will reveal the blasphemy of the old questions — it was an affront to the goodness and love of God which we know now overrides everything else. Face to face with God the whole situation appears different. It is important to recognize that the various words from the cross come from quite different presentations of the passion, but both presentations have their own validity. The cry of desolation in Mark and Matthew is not found in Luke or John. In Luke we find, 'Father, into thy hands I commit my spirit'; in John the triumphant cry, 'It is finished'. The absence of God and the presence of God. The agony of the world and the joy of the kingdom. The one does not do away with the other, but it does transform it.

Fifteen months ago the local convent invited all the residents of Selly Park to a carol service during the week after Christmas. I took Arthur along in his wheelchair. He loves singing and music. There in the chapel I was very conscious of his presence, especially since many people there did not know him and it is impossible to keep him quiet. In the chapel was a statue of Our Lady. Out of that combination of circumstances came this:

> Mary, my child's lovely.
> Is yours lovely too?
> Little hands, little feet.
> Curly hair, smiles sweet.
>
> Mary, my child's broken.
> Is yours broken too?
> Crushed by affliction,
> Hurt by rejection,
> Disfigured, stricken,
> Silent submission.
>
> Mary, my heart's bursting.
> Is yours bursting too?
> Bursting with labour, travail and pain.
> Bursting with agony, ecstacy, gain.
> Bursting with sympathy, anger, compassion.
> Bursting with praising Love's transfiguration.
>
> Mary, my heart's joyful.
> Is yours joyful too?

Further reflection on the theological implications of all this will be found in Part B.

Chapter 5

HOW ABOUT THE CHURCH?

It has always meant a great deal to me that Arthur is baptized. He will never be able to make his own response of faith, but his baptism as an infant means that he is a member of the body of Christ, and no one can take that away from him or exclude him. In recent controversies about the comparative claims of infant baptism and of believers' baptism, I have not hesitated to stress this. The idea of baptism in the New Testament is partly to do with the washing away of the old worldliness; but it is also about incorporation into the new humanity. In a missionary situation, of course this happened to believers; but in any event, it is not something we do ourselves, it is something done to us, just as ordination is not something we do ourselves — it is the act of the church in the name of God. My afflicted son belongs to Christ, not because he can profess his faith in him, but because Christ has accepted him.

But how has this worked out in practice? To what extent has it been possible to integrate him into the life of the church? We have to face up to the fact that the church is not and has never been perfect, for all its ideology and its high-flown doctrinal statements about itself. The church is a human institution which cannot but reflect the society to which it belongs. People find it difficult to accept oddities. Extreme differences in looks or behaviour or capabilities are difficult to integrate. On the whole my experience with Arthur has been very good, very positive. But it has hardly been possible for him to move up the normal rungs of the Sunday School. There are some situations and some kinds of services to which I could never take him. It is not so long since babies and toddlers got disapproving looks because they disturbed the silent meditation of serious worshippers — how much more a large child who won't keep quiet and makes odd noises? One of the liberating features of the independent black churches is the noise and exuberance of their worship, their acceptance of everyone of us, with joy and love and concern, Arthur included. There is no sense there of forcing Arthur on people who would rather not know and cannot cope. The same can be said of the local convent and of each of the Methodist churches with which we have been closely associated and where he has become known; though perhaps it says something about the inhibited society of white people that I have tended not to take him along when first going into a totally unfamiliar situation, whereas I have never hesitated to take him when paying a one-off visit to a black church with the Centre for Partnership.

Arthur began church life, like any other baby, in the creche; and there he stayed, for years and years. As things got more difficult in the 'middle period', his attendance became more erratic — it was easier to leave him at home except on the relatively rare occasions when Bob accompanied us. But he still came sufficiently regularly for us all to assume that he was acceptable in the familiar creche environment. Looking back I can see we expected too much. There came the day when the minister had to pay me a visit and gently point out that his size and his noise was more than the babies (or their mums) could cope with.

With my head I fully understood. I recognized the truth of what he was saying — indeed, I ought to have seen it myself. But in those days distress was never far below the surface, and although I knew it was unreasonable, I felt rejected because Arthur was rejected. Of course there were assurances that some solution would be found, that Arthur did belong; but the incident deepened the black hole, the sense of abandonment.

A few days later I was pushing Arthur up to the shops in his wheelchair, my heart very heavy. As we went past the Catholic church I noticed a priest coming towards us. He was hobbling, and to use the biblical term, had a withered arm and leg. When we met he stopped and spoke, first to me, then to Arthur. He only passed the time of day, and then said, 'How lovely to see him out and about!' After he had disappeared, it gradually dawned on me that he had embodied the acceptance of the church, indeed God's acceptance of Arthur and of me with him. The weight moved. The unreasonable reaction gave way to the more realistic perception of the situation.

So for the moment, Arthur's involvement with the church lapsed; but some months later, in association with the church anniversary weekend, an exhibition of local concerns was mounted. I arranged for a stand from the Birmingham Society for Mentally Handicapped Children, whose headquarters are in the locality. I took Arthur along and we manned the stand together. During the afternoon, one of the older members of the church came and insisted on staying with Arthur while I had a break and a cup of tea. It was on her initiative that Arthur was re-integrated into the life of the church. She and others formed a rota to sit with him in the manse after the Sunday school went out; he was to come into the first part of the service, like all the other children.

The first few Sundays were very hard. People were welcoming, always asked after him, totally accepting. But I still remember the self-consciousness, the worry over the fact that I could not keep him quiet. Yet there was the joy too. How much he loved the music and hymns! How much support unexpected people gave! I shall never forget what Flora Whitfield did, what she made possible. If it had not been for her I would never have been in a position years later to take Arthur to worship in black churches or anywhere else. When she was in the local hospice dying of cancer, I went to see her. Every time she asked after Arthur and rejoiced in any little progress or detail I could tell. Every time I came away deeply moved, most of all on the occasion when she asked after my progress towards ordination, and revealed she was praying for me. She did more than she knew in facilitating my path towards the ministry.

During the candidating process I affirmed that Arthur would be part of my ministry. During training that statement was fulfilled in quite unexpected ways. I spent some time gaining pastoral experience in circuit. I shall never forget the afternoon when I went visiting, and the first person I called on turned out to have a grandson with Down's Syndrome. We were able to share. The next call was to a council house where there lived a West Indian member of the congregation, Mrs Pemberton. I was shown into the front room, and conversation got off to rather a slow start. The room was full of photographs of her family, and we began to swap information about our children. She spoke of hers; I spoke of mine. When I mentioned Arthur and explained his condition, she suddenly said, 'I have a child like that too'. I found it difficult to piece together all she told me, but it turned out he had been in hospital for some years. He was a big lad, very spastic, impossible for her to handle. She had told no one at the church about him. She used to visit him; a friend from her husband's work had taken them over on a Sunday quite regularly. But now her husband was out of work. She couldn't get all the way to Kidderminster. She hadn't seen him since July. Gradually her pain and her questions — why do these things happen?

97

— came pouring out. My story was a catalyst for her story.

The next weekend was Easter weekend. I arranged to spend Easter Saturday driving her to Kidderminster to see her son. The way was familiar enough — Arthur and I had been many times to see our consultant. As it happened I had expected to be on my own that weekend — the family were going to my parents for Easter, while I stayed to fulfil my ministerial obligations. But in the event, Arthur still had both legs in plaster, it was impossible to take him to Belfast by public transport and I needed the car. Somehow I had to manage both Arthur and the Easter commitments at the church. For Good Friday my uncle was 'Arthur-sitter'. For Saturday and Sunday I had to take him along. So on Easter Saturday, he came in the car to Kidderminster, and we each met the other's son. She brought along a younger boy, about twelve, to visit his handicapped brother. It was a beautiful day, and on the way back we stopped at the Clent hills. We left Arthur in the car and walked up the hill a little way. Her boy rolled over and over on the grass with delight. No doubt it was an unusual experience for a young black from the inner city. And when we came down, she bought Arthur an ice-cream.

Easter day was memorable for many reasons. For 8 a.m. communion, I left Arthur in the vestry. But he joined the church breakfast, and Mrs Pemberton sat next to him and took a great delight in him. It was as though his presence liberated her, and she was able to take the lead in integrating him into the church family. He came into the family service later in the morning. To my delight and surprise, one member of the congregation pushed him up to the communion rail so that he too shared the blessing of the children. It was a moving moment when I layed my hand on his head — and not just for me. Arthur was part of my ministry that weekend.

Subsequently I was able to sort out arrangements for Mrs Pemberton to visit her son every other Sunday. Using the mobility allowance he has a right to, the hospital is able to finance a taxi once a fortnight to convey his mother and a friend there and back. It has become a shared joy for her and another church member. So through Arthur, we have both experienced what the church can be at its best, a community of love and care and support, a community without prejudice, without barriers, where all kinds of odd bits of humanity can find they have a place. It really can happen. The trouble is we are so inhibited, so fearful of testing it out, so prone to hide the vulnerable bits of ourselves. Yet before God, we are all equally vulnerable — it is no good pretending to him; and vulnerability shared in his name is the way to real human fellowship.

It was because I shared my vulnerability with that inner city church that things happened. I certainly gave myself to them, but I also received, immeasurably received. Preaching there was a different experience from preaching anywhere else, not because I used different material, but because the relationship was different. In most places where I preach people are more inhibited, more intimidated by who I am. There is the kind of respect which builds barriers. In the inner city my labels were almost meaningless. It was I, as a human being, who shared with other human beings. There was a different kind of respect on both sides, arising out of shared vulnerability. The sense that every single member of that very assorted congregation mattered and had a gift to contribute and that there was something about even the least to be respected, came across from the minister with whom I worked, and created an atmosphere and a level of relationship which I have scarcely encountered anywhere else. In the areas of society where many of us move, there is an atmosphere of competitiveness, and we are all scared of falling short. We dare not admit our own inferiority complexes. So we live on the surface and do not really share. Those of us who are privileged in our society think we ought to give to the less privileged, but so easily that becomes charity at arms length, or a sense of disabling guilt because we don't do enough, or patronage. What we need to do is to receive. We need to admit our vulnerability and inadequacy and need. Then we can receive the gospel, we can receive the ministry of others. To receive from someone is to accord them a deeper respect, and to do them far more good than to give them our charity. This I have learned not only in that inner city church, but through the Centre for Partnership between Black and White. In both settings I have given, of course, by teaching, preaching, pastoral visiting, and so on; but in each I have received more than I have given. This, it seems to me, puts a different complexion on 'Mission alongside the Poor', and on 'liberation theology'. So often the message comes across as a condemnation of the affluent. It should be heard as an invitation: 'Come and receive a different perspective on life. Come and re-discover the simple values. Come and enter into fellowship with us. You will be enriched. You will find your real self. You will find Christ as you have never known him before. You will find the church being itself, where there are no distinctions between Jew or Greek, male or female, slave or free, rich or poor, black or white, handicapped or intelligent, old or young, but all are one in Christ.' I feel privileged to have had the opportunity to learn of these things.

It is through such experiences that I found the inner strength and serenity to learn chaplaincy work by being placed at the local Hospital for Mentally Handicapped Adults. A few years ago I still found the presence of handicapped people *en masse* profoundly distressing. At times I even had to pluck up courage to go to events at my own son's school. But I had reached the point where I felt I had worked through all the hang-ups and perhaps had something to give. I found again that I was receiving more than I gave. To be obliged to switch off from all the rush of teaching and doing things once a week, and just go and be with people for whom life was basic and simple, for some of whom verbal communication was difficult or impossible, became profoundly important. It was a sharing of peace and friendship and simplicity, entering a community in which there was a remarkable atmosphere of simple gratitude, a capacity to receive, a delight in little treasures, like photographs, shown off with great pride. A little old lady, deaf and speechless, played peep-bo with a cuddly scarf, and the two of us were close in our smiles and embraces of affection. Another more capable lady took me into her room and showed me all her things, spoke of particular things Sister had done for her, 'She's very good, you know', pointed to a poster of Our Lady and said, 'She's my friend'. Another old lady spent all her time knitting, mostly blankets and clothes for her doll; the doll was her child, spoken of with the affection and annoyance of a mother, 'She's naughty sometimes, you know'. They shared themselves with me, each a character in his or her own right in spite of decades of institutionalization. Then there was Denis. Some of the men were bright old things who could run errands and reminisce to your heart's content. Others were stuck in the home for one reason or another. Sister suggested I might take one or two who did not get out much, to the Club, the Hospital's social centre. Denis had no speech and seemed to sit all day with a rather glum look on his face, playing with his fingers. I suggested we might go out, and immediately he got up, clearly understanding language even if he had none. We went to his room and he led me to

101

ing that here were some of the most vulnerable persons in our society, yet each was a self, each had value, and before God we were all equally vulnerable human beings in need of his grace. Even more moving was sharing in the administration of the sacrament. The rush to the rail, the grateful 'thank you', the simple receptivity, seemed to bring a new depth to what we shared together. There was something more significant here than grasping the right teaching about what a sacrament is, or arguing whether the elements are or are not the body and blood of Christ. To receive with that simple desire and genuine gratitude, trusting that here is the bread of life . . . would that we were all like that every time we communicated. There is a mystery here. Protestant insistence on belief and understanding our commitment, the sort of thing that fuels the demand for believers' baptism rather than infant baptism, misses out on the inarticulate but profound response that children, like the handicapped, may make. Not that I would go back on all I have said about the urgent necessity that Christians love God with their minds, and not just their feelings; those of us with intelligence have an obligation to use our gifts and not be fearful of facing questions. But we need the witness of the simple too. There has always been tension in the life of the church between intellectuals and simple believers — the suspicion and hostility faced by the early theologian Origen in third-century Alexandria are evidence enough. But in spite of the fact he was drummed out of the city by the bishop and had to set up his Christian philosophical school elsewhere, one of Origen's arguments for the truth of Christianity was that whereas philosophy had only made the elite good, Christian faith had lifted people of all levels of society and of every different type and race to a 'philosophical' way of life. Perhaps we would not want to put it quite like that, but it is important we respect each other across the divides and recognize we all have a contribution to make. Just as male needs female, rich needs poor, white needs black, so intellectuals need the simple, and vice versa in each case. The church is itself when it bridges all these gaps and tensions between people of different kinds. Someone from a very ordinary church congregation said to me at the end of one service, 'You are not like most theologians'. I suppose she meant it as a compliment, but I felt like retorting, 'What on earth do you think theologians are like? Don't trust stereotypes — they're always misleading.'

One of the greatest joys of worship in the Hospital was the participation of my youngest son. William came along on one occasion to help teach a new song. After that he came again and again, because he wanted to. He loved the handicapped people. He loved to be worshipping with them. On the last occasion he was a willing assistant as I tried to set up an *ad hoc* simple drama to get the point of the lesson across, acting as page and so steering the volunteers who participated in the right direction. Later in the service, I noticed that one handicapped person in whom I had some interest, but with whom I had failed to make any meaningful contact, either verbally or physically, leant across and asked my son to find his place in the hymnbook. I was deeply touched.

There is something about the communion of saints, the fellowship of all God's people, transcending space and time, which comes across to me here. There in that church is gathered a group of people who are truly marginalized in our society. How far they should be is a question to which I wish to return in the next chapter. Yet they share a common pattern of worship with the rest of the church, they offer intercessions for the world, they are a priestly community within the hospital praying for the community in which they live and work. Most of us outside are totally unaware of this. The church in general has woken up, at least in its prayer life, to the needs of the Third World, the crises that the media present us with, and so on. But on our doorsteps are worlds we know nothing about, communities that could enrich us, communities that need our prayers and support, groups that are in the world yet not of the world, to which access is a privilege, but we pass by the gate with averted eyes. I feel I would like to go to the average prosperous congregation and say, 'Come with me. Come and see this thing that has come to pass. Come and rejoice. Come and share. You could even help a bit with finding the place in the hymnbook. But you would receive more than you give. You won't find peace and quiet for silent mediation. You'll find a lot of noise and unpredictable movement, an unfamiliar atmosphere. But if your eyes and your hearts are open, you will find something quite extraordinary, a miracle of grace. But even if you don't come, it is still there — part of the communion of saints.'

I suppose one thing I am trying to say through this account is that the church has been criticizing itself for too long, and it ought to start celebrating its unsung and unremarkable achievements. The trouble is that the faults of the church are so obvious — the gap between its ideals and the reality is so glaring. But the other trouble is that most of us do not have our eyes open to see the miracles of grace. They are to be found in such ordinary, unremarkable, simple things that we do not even notice. We think our worship is dull, and miss the movement of the Spirit in the secret places, the everyday saints, who are there among us but we dismiss them as 'old so-and-so'. In my experience the church is capable of transcending the divisions in our society, it is capable of integrating the odd and unacceptable, it is more sensitive to basic human values than wider society. It can act as leaven, and we should not disparage this. Maybe we all need to go on a voyage of exploration into unlikely places to meet unlikely people — not the great ones of the world but the marginalized and afflicted who will teach us what true human values are. Certainly it is Jean Vanier, the founder of the L'Arche communities where Christians live with handicapped people, who writes with the greatest depth these days about community life.[16] But the purpose of such a journey would be to open our eyes, so that we can return to the place where we belong and begin to discern those values where we are.

The values we may discern are to do with both the individual and the community. Handicapped people are all very different from one another. No two persons have the same combination of handicaps. No two persons have the same capabilities or the same personality. Individuality is even more marked than it is in a group of so-called 'normal' people. And as I said earlier, this is the way these people are. Acceptance of people as they are is one of the values to be discovered. Identification with other people is another. In the handicapped we can discern the human condition. We are none of us 'perfect'. We share the same basic needs — food, drink, sleep, love. . . . We have the same instinctive desire for life, the same ultimate end in death, the same frailty, the same vulnerability. We need to sense this identification with those who reveal, sometimes very poignantly, what the human condition really is. We are all in need of grace, and to join in confession with those who cannot always be regarded as totally responsible for all their actions and yet feel shame and regret, is to be reminded we are in the same case, that we need absolution too. And it is in that identification that community begins to be realized, because we learn to receive as well as give, and the barriers of self-consciousness, the fear of inferiority, the patronizing

16 Jean Vanier, *Community and Growth*, Darton, Longman and Todd 1979.

tone of superiority, are melted away. There is profound communication in a touch, and none is excluded. Prayer is turned into thanksgiving instead of desperate petition.

It is when we begin to see that these are the most important values — not achievement, or success, or prosperity, or even do-gooding — that we can discern the presence of God's kingdom in our midst, at any rate in anticipation. This is a 'foretaste of the heavenly banquet'. The Bible looks forward to God re-creating the world, resurrecting humanity to a new life, in some sense continuous with this, and yet transformed. That I think is where we can find a true Christian hope for the future. I do not think we have immortal souls. I think we are frail creatures of dust and everyone of us needs renewal and healing, re-making in fact. We are in the same case as the handicapped. Our present existence is the 'seed' of a new existence: 'Someone will ask, "How are the dead raised? With what kind of body do they come?"'... What you sow is not the body which is to be, but a bare kernel.... So it is with the resurrection of the dead. What is sown is perishable, what is raised is imperishable.... It is sown in weakness, it is raised in power.... Lo, I tell you a mystery. We shall not all sleep, but we shall all be changed....' It would be worth reading carefully the whole of I Cor. 15.

I dare not speculate what my ultimate destiny may be, still less what Arthur's may be; but I do think that there will be continuity between what we are now and what we will be then. Arthur is a whole person as much as I am. I am a handicapped person as much as he is. We will both be renewed. And we both have some inkling in the present of what that renewed life will be like, because we experience it in the fellowship and sacraments of the church. Such a hope can hardly be expressed in words, but we may make some attempt through parables and images drawn from our experience of situations in which each unique individual matters and yet is transcended in the whole community:

A party invitation! the heavenly feast!
Who'll be there?
Everyone's invited, even the least.
I've nothing to wear . . .
A special robe is provided, designed for you.
Look at my hair!
Don't worry — they'll give you a bath and a fine hair-do.
No gift to bear . . .
Just bring your musical instrument to play.
Arthur can't share.
Everyone will participate in some way.
Stuck in his chair?
Somehow he'll be fitted to play his role.
Will people stare?
No, no. He'll take his part in the joyful whole.
He'll be aware?
Everyone will respond and give of their best.
   Each has some flair.
   The conductor, you see, will be a special guest.
   Under his care
   The entire ensemble will play together as one.
That'll be rare.
That is how Christ will complete the work begun
   Suffering in prayer.
   There'll be music beyond any music heard on earth
   Throbbing the air.
   There'll be bread and wine. New life will be brought to birth.
   God will be there.
   You'll finally understand his infinite grace.
   There's plenty to spare.
Will we be able to see him face to face?
Look — if you dare!

Chapter 6

DOES SOCIETY CARE?

On that occasion when I broke down at a school medical, the doctor said to me, 'You think this child is all your own responsibility, don't you? He isn't. He is society's responsibility. Society needs handicap.'

I have often since reflected on that amazing statement: society needs handicap. Why does society need handicap? I guess it is easier to answer the question from a Christian point of view than any other. Handicapped people remind us that life is not all go-getting and individual achievement. There are more fundamental human values. Handicap demands mutual support, a sense of communal sharing. Handicap fosters compassion and helpfulness, care and concern. It challenges our selfishness and our ambition and sectional loyalties. Society needs handicap.

But for the most part our society does not want to know of these things. Our society is really only interested in achievers; it admires the handicapped who achieve, like the blind student at university, or the wheelchair-bound marathon-runner. All of us are affected by these values. Most people who deal with the mentally handicapped look for the small triumphs, and achieving the maximum potential of a handicapped person is regarded as the aim by good parents and good professionals. There is pressure all the time to be triumphant. Professionals and parents alike want things that work, believing that progress and self-help is enhancing dignity, and increasing social acceptability. By and large we cannot admit lack of achievement, and as a society, we cannot cope with those whose handicap *is* lack of achievement, for whatever reason. This applies not only to those with less than average IQ, but to those who grow up disadvantaged and deprived. Non-achievers are marginalized in our society.

It seems to me that this implies a distortion of values. Does self-help, if it has been mechanically drilled into behaviour and is merely the response of an automaton, actually increase dignity? Isn't a relaxed and caring relationship, an ability to let the person be himself, a greater value? Isn't behaviour modification, however successful in increasing social acceptability, a way of manipulation and a denial of true humanity? Is achievement the be-all and end-all? What kind of triumph is appropriate? Society measures triumph in terms of preserving life at all costs, developing full potential, overcoming the odds? But might not the real triumph be the ability to receive from one another, to discover interdependence, to find values which make success and death equally irrelevant? Should we not allow the handicapped to stimulate questioning about the value of autonomy and conformity, and look for oᵗ ᵢer forms of transformation? The inbuilt attitudes of society are shown up by this 'activist' response to handicap.

Other social conditions have produced quite different reactions. My attention was drawn recently to the comments of the mediaeval poet, William Langland, in *Piers Plowman*;[17] for him the 'lunatics' who take no thought for the morrow, and do not kow-tow to anyone are 'God's apostles', the only incorruptible members of society. They are to be valued and given hospitality. They perform a very special kind of service to society, in being a comment upon the attitudes of everyone else. It reminds me of the long-standing, but very odd, Christian tradition that some are called to be 'fools for Christ': there were those who quite

---

[17] *Piers Plowman*, CText IX. 105-118; translation H. W. Wells, Passus VII. 130ff., Classics of Western Spirituality. Sheed & Ward 1973. I am grateful to Valerie Edden for drawing my attention to this passage.

deliberately concealed themselves in the guise of witless and irresponsible beggars, living on trust, as a way of ascetic discipleship. Perhaps there is something here that our society needs to rediscover, the value of fools, the contribution of the handicapped to an alternative set of human values. Our society is not good at valuing the non-achiever, nor at integrating the odd and different.

Indeed, public attitudes often leave much to be desired. Before I go any further I must stress that our experience with Arthur has usually been that the general public rises to the occasion. Taking our family across to Northern Ireland was always a bit of a caper. We generally drove to Stranraer, left our car parked there, and travelled as foot passengers across on the ferry. That meant getting children and luggage and Arthur in his wheelchair up gang planks. Invariably some fellow traveller would turn up trumps and give assistance. But I guess we are lucky. The handicap is so obvious, and the wheelchair tells its own story. Other families tell different stories. What do you do if your child looks normal, is a big teenager, but behaves oddly in public? Can you cope with sitting on a beach while everyone stares or avoids you? One of the problems of our society is the anonymity that comes with crowds. The village simpleton grew up in a small community where everyone knew him. He would be greeted by the locals, and if necessary reminded to button up his fly. But a new housing development in the village brings strangers who call in the police. Let me quote from an article in the magazine of the Catholic Handicapped Children's Fellowship.[18] It was written by a helper at one of their summer camps and told of the impact of an incident in the local town:

[18] Winifred Johnson, 'The Incident that Removed My Depression', *The Fellowship Review*, the annual magazine of the Catholic Handicapped Childrens' Fellowship, 1971-72, p. 6.

One morning we took six children with us . . . We went to a
nearby cafe and bought coffee and milkshakes . . . A family
— father, mother, and three children — came in and sat at
the next table. A good-looking family nicely dressed and
well-spoken. My six boys waved and smiled, and went on
noisily sucking the milkshakes through straws. Suddenly I
became aware of a low and intense whispered conversation
going on at the next table. When I turned round the
whispering stopped abruptly but I saw an expression in the
eyes of the mother and father that even now makes me go
cold when I think of it. The expression was one of disgust
and anger and it was directed at my children. The mother
said, 'They shouldn't bring children like that into here.'
The remark was addressed to her husband but she was
watching me. . . Later in the day, I told the camp organiser
about the incident and he said, 'I'm afraid this sort of thing
happens all too often. People want handicapped children to
be kept conveniently out of sight. Well-looked after, of
course (after all we're not Nazis) but out of the way.'

The question whether society can cope with handicap is
a serious one. It is all the more serious now that the policy
of the government and many professionals is what they call
'community care'. What I fear is that this is a high-sounding
ideal which is simply a way of making cuts in services,
putting pressure on already hard-pressed families and
exposing the most vulnerable people in our society to all
kinds of dangers — like being picked up by the police,
because they are inadequate to cope with the complexities
of life in a community that is *not* a community but a vast
conglomeration of people with all kinds of explosive tensions. Society cannot absorb the oddity unless it has a
cohesiveness and stability of its own which certainly does
not exist in our modern cities. Only this month there is an
article in the Mencap magazine, *Parents' Voice*,[19] describing

[19] Margaret Flynn, 'Community Backlash', *Parents' Voice*, Journal of the Royal
Society for Mentally Handicapped Children and Adults vol. 34.1, May 1984,
pp. 16-17

how a few mentally handicapped people were placed in an ordinary house in the community, with marvellous back-up from social workers and others, but their lives were ruined by the local kids following them about, name-calling, and by a nasty hard-core who obtained access to the house, and egged on by the helpless distress of its occupants, played havoc with its contents, eventually setting fire to it. This is a particularly horrifying case, but the policy of emptying the hospitals has thrown up many local stories of public lack of acceptance, inadequate supervision, exploitation, and so on.

This is not to underestimate the very great strides forward that have been made. Public awareness and acceptance is far higher than it was, as a result of the public relations efforts of Mencap and its local societies, as a result of some very sensitive documentaries on television, and many other enlightened things, like the willingness of parents to live their lives as normally as possible and not hide their shame in a back bedroom. The way in which even mildly handicapped people were shoved into institutions, shut away from society's gaze, was a scandal. I have now met old people of 60, 70, even 80, who were treated like this, and know it. They tell of their regimented lives, marched to the fields to work every day, marched to the church on a Sunday — all because they had failed to learn to read. Is it any wonder that the mood in the old peoples' home at the hospital is one of gratitude — for the relaxed atmosphere, the end of custodial care? For the more able, the encouragement to live in hostels and manage their own lives is in many cases undoubtedly right. But I doubt if the hospitals will ever be emptied. For one thing, the advantageous economics is not as obvious as all that: for a while I served on the Committee of Birmingham Mencap which ran its first Home, and I was horrified at the level of staffing costs for the care of only seven handicapped persons. Twenty-four hour coverage for those who need supervision, even though these residents needed no nursing care, is astronomical; and the same staff could have supervised twice the number in a larger building. Besides, there are many who need a restricted environment where they have security. I vividly recall an article in *Parents' Voice*[20] written by a mother whose daughter was being discharged from a hospital into the community, expressing her feeling that this was not an enlightened and progressive move at all. Her daughter had thrived in the context of a 'campus' where she could wander round in safety, she had thrived in a community large enough yet small enough for her to belong and still have freedom to form a wide circle of acquaintances. Outside the hospital she would lose freedom, she would need protection and she would be restricted in her relationships.

And finally, there will always be the severely handicapped who need nursing care. Most of the imaginative schemes, like those of the Home Farm Trust, cream off the more able. And a hard core is left. The old subnormality hospital has had a bad press and it is not surprising that a parents' organization like Mencap should press for a more domestic scale and a more normal living environment. But I do not think it will ever be possible to eliminate some such protected community for those who have no family that can cope and cannot learn to cope for themselves even with social-work backup. Nor are such places any longer what the horror stories have suggested. The biggest threat is that the new fad for 'community care' will deprive them of the finances needed to go on improving the quality of life for

[20] Hazel West, 'Care in Whose Community?', *Parents' Voice*, vol. 33.3, September 1983.

residents and staff alike. Society's responsibility is to provide adequate services for its most vulnerable members. I resent every government promise to cut taxes. It can only mean that the weakest are deprived while the strongest prosper.

One of the curious things about joining the chaplaincy staff at the hospital was that I suddenly found myself on the professionals' side, as it were, rather than that of parent. Staff talked to me as a novice on the scene, unaware of my long-standing connections with it. They were anxious to explain their work; they shared their positive commitment to improving life for the residents left in the hospital, to providing family support — the changing concept of the hospital's role. But the thing that came across most forcibly was the seriousness of the staff situation in the face of current cuts. Young committed staff were disillusioned. They had been trained to help these people help themselves, not just watch over them. But helping people to help themselves takes time and effort, and as staff numbers are cut to the minimum, it has to go. Several spoke bitterly of being forced back into a 'minding' role whether they like it or not. Two young male staff were training for other employment — they wanted out, not because they did not like the work — if there had been any prospect of doing the job properly and building a career, they would have stayed. Morale of staff like these was low. Society is simply not bearing the cost of handicap. It does not want to know. It wants to get rid of potentially first class communities because of the scandals of the past. It wants care on the cheap.

Such places are potentially first class communities involving staff as well as residents, and these days they are multiracial into the bargain — a microcosm of what society might be. However low staff morale seemed to be, the sheer devotion to the job and to the people was impressive. The effort put into Christmas, into outings, into holidays away from the hospital at the seaside, into community-building was remarkable. There were many who in spite of everything could not imagine doing any other job; the Sister running the home for disturbed women who used to work in a bank and would never go back; the secretary who had once worked in industry and wrote in the hospital magazine:

> Whilst it would not be true to say that I did not enjoy my work in industry, I must admit that I find the work I am presently involved in much more satisfying . . . I have found the atmosphere throughout the hospital noticeably more relaxed and informal . . . (Problems) seem to be handled in a more calm and positive manner. . . . Before working here, I had never given much thought to the fact that the hospital never closes which, when you think of it, is an achievement in itself. In industry most firms (are) . . . a 'ghost town' for the weekend . . . Industry is run on business lines whereas the hospital, as I see it, operates like a huge family unit. I am glad that I am now part of the family. . . .
>
> Whilst we are all very much aware of the need for industry, it is sad to think that not everyone in industry is aware of hospitals like this one.[21]

Society's responsibility is to support, and pay for, the necessary sheltered communities for those of the handicapped who will never cope elsewhere.

But this need not and should not be a shutting of the unacceptable out of the way. There are all kinds of ways in which it is possible for people to be involved, and the hospitals no longer have shut gates. Churches can invite residents to socials, and they certainly enjoy a trip out. Volunteers can go in and make friends, adopt a resident

---

[21] *Link*, Monyhull Staff Magazine, June 1983; Contribution by Norma Meredith, Secretary to the Nursing Officer.

and keep in touch. The hospitals can be integrated more into normal society — indeed they already are, as the city spreads to engulf what was once buried in the country. People are more aware of the handicapped in their midst, and more are living in small homes and hostels among ordinary people. But there is still an awful lot of education to be done: the most well-meaning people confuse mental handicap and mental illness. (In case the distinction is not clear, mental handicap is a permanent condition caused by physical damage to the brain; mental illness is a psychological condition which may be temporary and curable.) There is an instinctive fear of the odd and unfamiliar. Most parents have felt at some time or other that they have had to brazen it out. Yet if we do not insist on doing so, people will never get used to the idea that the handicapped belong; they belong to us all.

There is another context in which parents often have to brazen it out. That is in dealing with the professionals delegated by society actually to handle the problem of handicap. For the most part the extended family has disappeared, neighbours live in their little boxes with their own busy lives, and there is no community support which is not professionally provided by health visitors, doctors, social workers and schools, and the bureaucracy that dishes out allowances. Again I must insist that on the whole we have had excellent relations with those immediately concerned with Arthur. The school has been marvellous, always helpful, always willing to listen. Our social worker has gone out of her way to obtain suitable accommodation for Arthur when we needed a break. What I am about to say must be read with that background in mind. But the ambiguities in our experience need to be brought out, because there are so many without our advantages who must feel these things even worse, and who do not have the ability to speak up for themselves or articulate their difficulties. It is precisely the people most in need who find the whole institutionalized palaver of benefit offices and the NHS most intimidating.

Let us begin with allowances and benefit offices. A year or so ago we had a letter from the DHSS: unless they heard from us within so many days, Arthur's mobility allowance book would be made out in his own name, since he would be sixteen next birthday and eligible to draw it himself. Needless to say I immediately wrote and informed them that he was incapable of managing his own affairs and could not sign his own name. Weeks and weeks later I received a notification from the local office demanding that I present myself for an interview. Wondering what was up, I duly presented myself. After some delay I was summoned into a private office and asked why I had requested to have the book made payable to myself. I said exactly what I had said in my letter. The official went off and fetched a form. She filled it in for me, and then asked me to sign it. Some time later we had a letter requesting a doctor's certificate to confirm what I had said about Arthur's condition. We complied with the request and waited further weeks. Arthur passed his birthday and the allowance book ran out. Eventually we rang the office to find the certificate had been buried in a file and not forwarded to the Mobility Allowance office at all. Then through the post, in spite of it all, came an allowance book made out in Arthur's name! By the time the appropriate allowance book arrived, we were owed an enormous sum in back payments.

All this palaver was not a lot of bother to us, but I put myself in the shoes of others who depend on such allowances. For many people coping with the kind of handicap implied by the provision of mobility allowance, a journey to the office would have been a major undertaking, and it was totally unnecessary. I can well imagine the nervousness induced in many people at the mere summons: what was wrong? Had they revealed something which jeopardised the allowance? Besides it is demeaning to be treated as incapable of filling in a form for oneself; no doubt some clients cannot, but that does not mean depriving everybody of their competence and dignity. I have enough self-regard to put up with this sort of thing, but I resent it on behalf of others. I am happy enough to accept the principle that evidence be provided that my statement about my son was true; no doubt there are parents who would exploit their own children. But I do object to the total waste of postage and time, both mine and that of the office staff. Why could they not have dealt with the situation in one go, sending the request for a medical certificate and the form to sign straight away and cutting out all the to-ing and fro-ing? And the delay — it didn't matter to us, but what about those who depend on their allowances? What about those who have no telephone and not enough confidence to pursue 'them'? The bureaucracy needs to rediscover a human face, and a more efficient procedure. Anyone would think ours was an exceptional case, but it must arise countless times. And the bureaucracy is efficient enough in pulling its money back: before we got the book for Arthur's invalidity pension, the family allowance book was called in and adjusted. Great care is taken to ensure that no one gets anything they are not entitled to.

Talking of that feature leads me on to another story — this time it is about the NHS. Arthur's incontinence has always been with us, and the way we have handled it has really been an extension of the babyhood practice of using nappies. We are geared up to it with suitable washing machines and drying arrangements. But plastic pants became a problem: he got too big for the typical baby-pairs you can get in chemists' shops. We heard from other parents about the supply of disposable rolls and plastic pants. I asked our social worker. She said I could call in at the Community Health centre and pick up what we needed. I could and did. There was a funny old man who would just take your word for it, fill a plastic sack with rolls, produce a couple of pairs of plastic holders and all was fine. We went about every three months. We only needed rolls for school.

Then came the cuts. So what did they do? They employed a secretary to check up on every issue from the Community Health stores. The secretary must have cost more than they saved. The informal arrangement no longer worked. A call from the social worker got us on the list, but then they would only give us a couple of rolls at a time, and we were lucky to get any plastic pants. There was no way we could call frequently enough to get enough rolls for school use. School kept pressing. Other parents were on the laundry service; they had a regular supply delivered every week. Why didn't we apply? Eventually I tracked down the District Nurse and a formal application was put in. We were put on a two year waiting list. Think of it — people coping with incontinent old people on a two year waiting list! They're likely to die before they get what they need. It is now more than two years and we have not yet seen any sign of the laundry service. Mind you, we have given up.

Professionals are always telling us to keep fighting for our rights, but we have got better uses of our time and energies. What concerns me is not our particular situation, but what it reveals about the stupidity of the whole set up, what it reveals about the hardships more vulnerable people must suffer. And this is supposed to be a caring society. Those who need the care are subject to suspicion and discouragement. They are exposed to unnecessary indignities — like the time my husband and I were sent separate bills to cover the parental contribution to Arthur's care. I hear people from disadvantaged backgrounds, immigrant groups, crying out at the way they are treated and saying this society is racist; I tell them it is not just those with the 'wrong' colour skin who suffer in this way in our society. It should not simply be interpreted as racist. Granted that it is worse for them at times because of racist attitudes, it is still a fact that even people like us, white, Anglo-Saxon, Protestant, comfortable, middleclass and articulate, are subject to being treated as non-persons when we present our vulnerable face to officialdom. There is something about the way state services are organized which creates an 'us' and 'them' situation which is profoundly alienating. I am glad that I have experienced something of this, and can stand with at least a small measure of understanding alongside the real poor and inadequates in our society. It is time we realized just how uncaring and inhuman our institutions are. It is time Socialists realized that this is what their ideals have produced — it has gone bad on them. It is time Conservatives realized that cuts have hurt the most vulnerable members of society whatever they say, and that stopping waste has created waste, and hardship. It is since they came to power that supplies for incontinence have mushroomed in Boots and in chemists' shop windows. At last we can get what we need — by paying for it. Society may need handicap, but it will not bear the cost of handicap. The unfortunate are made to feel that they are to blame for their misfortune.

What about medical services and doctors? I have already expressed my anger at the way the case was handled in the beginning. What more is there to say? When we moved to Birmingham, the health visitor appeared on our doorstep before Arthur and I had arrived — at least the grapevine worked! She was the first person we saw when we were able to return from his first spell in hospital, in Belfast. Still sore from the experience in Cambridge, I asked her if she could recommend an understanding GP. She indicated that she was not allowed to, and dropped a name. Even though we have moved away from that area of Birmingham, we have remained with that practice, and we have never had anything but understanding and support from the doctors themselves. The practice has from time to time employed 'dragons' as receptionists — but once that gauntlet has been run things have been splendid. Early on we were not only referred to appropriate consultants, but put in touch with a friend of one of the doctors who was concerned with special education. It was in this way that we were introduced to the Doman-Delacato method and encouraged to begin a regular programme of stimulation. From this General Practice we have had wise and helpful advice.

Hospitals have been another matter. I do not think I have ever felt more vulnerable than when attending clinics with Arthur. Our recent experience has been better, I must say. The consultant now takes care to book our relatively infrequent appointments at the end of the clinic so that I can take him after school; by then things are quiet and we usually have no wait. But when he was young, and difficult, I can remember hours of waiting, with no facilities for putting him on the floor to roll around. He would get tired of sitting on my knee, he would get fractious, his crying would start. I became a helpless object at the beck and call of busy nurses, who would demand that he be undressed and weighed, that such and such be done, and everything just got him more overtired and more difficult. Occasionally I met with kindness and understanding, but that would make me feel even more like weeping. Then there were the weeks he was in hospital with eczema, and I in an advanced state of pregnancy, sat by his bedside, trying to persuade him to sleep, protecting him from nurses who wanted to force him into their routine and had no appreciation of the particular difficulties of this particular child, who was still very much a baby though almost two. I shall not easily forget the moment when a fellow-parent came out to the Out-patients hall, where I was eating my snack lunch, to tell me that the minute I had left, the staff had woken Arthur to feed him — after I had spent all morning trying to get him relaxed and calm enough to drop off. He would not feed when overtired anyway. Maybe I was over-protective and over-worried, but we lived with the problem, and I knew the number of hours he was capable of crying, and the number of hours he would refuse to sleep, and how difficult he was to feed, and how impossible it was to force him out of his routine into any other. I was up against the inflexibility of institutions, and the rules of a skin ward that could make no allowance for the other problems a patient might have. Those were exhausting weeks.

And the consultants? Two have been remarkable, our present one and one on whose list we have not been for years and years, but she still recognizes us, still greets Arthur if she happens to see him in the clinic. She even knew me when we happened to be sitting one behind the other at a concert in the Town Hall — without Arthur, of course. She was kindness and helpfulness personified. But in the early days we sometimes saw her, and sometimes someone else. I still remember with vividness the day when one of the other consultants just bluntly said, 'He really is very handi-capped, you know. You will have to think about putting him into an institution.' I can't describe how I felt. No one should make remarks like that without knowing how the particular mother thinks and feels. It was callous and unwarranted.

Then there was that other consultant who said, 'If you don't get him off the bottle, he'll never develop the facial muscles to talk.' Talking — what a hope! How unrealistic could you get! Yet he put me in a panic, caused me to withdraw the bottle completely in despair of ever weaning him gradually, and compounded our problems. Something like that needed far more talking through, far more careful advice. On another occasion the same man said, 'You must never let the normal children be sacrificed for the handicapped one.' Well, yes. I have said the same myself earlier in this book. But at the time it really upset me. It seemed to imply a callousness towards Arthur which I simply could not take. Every one of my children mattered, Arthur included.

If only people knew what their casual words can do to others. And it is particularly the case when a doctor or someone in that sort of relationship with a patient or client says things. To the professional this is just one case among hundreds. To the person on the receiving end, it is the moment for which they have made a special and sometimes difficult journey, the moment for which they may have been waiting for a long time, the moment of anxiety, perhaps of hope that something helpful will be done or said. One is like putty, like a suppliant, a helpless, vulnerable bit of humanity with the thing that most distresses there, the subject of discussion. If only the professionals could remember that. Even the best can inadvertently hurt, like the first time the social worker spoke of taking Arthur into care. . . . My stomach turned over. Of course it is the professional jargon — but it has such connotations in our society, implying inadequacy in the mother. . . . She was a wonderful social worker, who took enormous trouble to help us, always encouraged us to accept relief and help whatever our anxieties or hesitation to ask too much, always fought for places in hostels for Arthur even when our own local authority had none and he had to go elsewhere, backed us up in an unpleasant interchange with a hostel warden (a couple of years later, he was taken to court and his hostel closed in the midst of a public scandal — what a world we live in!) . . . She was a marvellous social worker, yet that simple phrase rubbed salt in the wound. I know of occasions when I myself have said things I have immediately wished unsaid, or later deeply regretted. I become more and more convinced that we need the old proverbs of the biblical wisdom literature that warn of the dangers of the loose tongue: a gentle tongue is a tree of life, but perverseness in it breaks the spirit; pleasant words are like a honeycomb, but a whisperer separates close friends; the tongue is like a fire — no human being can tame the tongue, a restless evil, full of deadly poison. . . . We all need to watch our words. Even the best of the professionals need to hear how vulnerable their clients are.

Patients, or clients, are vulnerable partly because they are in a position in which they surrender their autonomy. They have to submit to advice from so-called 'experts', and in the process they can easily find themselves made to feel in need of help, therefore incompetent, therefore guilty. It is the hardest thing in the world to ask for help because it means a loss of self-sufficiency, a loss of self-esteem, a loss of dignity. One of the sad things in my experience of being on the other side, was to hear professionals criticizing parents. Now it is true that parents over-protect and suffocate with their love, and no doubt it is frustrating to spend all day trying to wean someone out of an unacceptable habit, only to have it encouraged when he goes home. But parents need to be affirmed. One of the encouraging things about more recent trends is the fact that professionals are recognizing that the parent is the expert on any particular child, and a more consultative role, an enabling role, is the professional's new self-understanding.

But even this needs to be handled carefully. In our depressing 'middle' period, we rather lost energy and certainly lost the 'I will do anything' attitude. We had a new baby to cope with. Arthur was a problem. I was working full time. It was so well-meaning to put pressure on me to join a parents' group, but at the time it really did have the effect of multiplying our problems and increasing the tensions. Somehow we were made to feel we ought to be doing more; but I was so drained I could not muster the strength. Going out to the group was an extra pressure, and usually left me more depressed. There are times when the help offered is unacceptable. It made me feel more vulnerable.

Yet over the three years the group met — I think it was once a month — it began to dawn on me that actually I was contributing. I was able to make some suggestions that helped other parents. I was able to listen to people whose problems were different from mine, and so our mutual problem-situations were put into different perspective — like the day one of the other couples raised the problem of shaving, and a whole new dimension opened up which we had not — and happily still have not — had to face with Arthur. Getting his hair cut is bad enough! Other parents drew my attention to services available, like the Community Health supplies for incontinence. I was able to obtain special equipment for teaching self-feeding. What was happening was that the competence and experience of parents was being facilitated and affirmed. My attitude to the group began to change. I guess if it had been presented to me not as something to help me help Arthur, and therefore as an extra guilt-producing pressure I could not cope with, but as a chance to help other parents, as an affirmation of my value to others because of my experience, I would have approached the whole thing in a different frame of mind. It is easier to help than to be helped. It takes an awful lot of humility to admit your need of help and receive it with gratitude. Being on the receiving end can be a very demeaning thing, and that I suppose is why the disadvantaged in our society are so profoundly alienated, and see government agencies, and town halls, whatever their political coloration, as 'them' ranged against 'us'.

This is the background against which the success of 'self-help' groups must be seen. Handicap has spawned a large number in our society: Spastics, Down's Syndrome, Muscular Dystrophy, Mencap, etc. These groups are important for all kinds of reasons. Some I have already indicated — the sheer getting-together of parents with pre-school handicapped children. To that should be added the provision of a social life for handicapped families who want it. Every Saturday there is a social at the Birmingham Society; there is dancing, a bar. We are not the sort to enjoy that sort of social interchange, but it is a vital service for many families who can go along all together, handicapped member included, and know they can have a good time with friends. Then there are the teenage clubs and other provisions for handicapped youngsters. Again we have never felt that Arthur could really benefit from this, especially after being out at school all day. But for most people such services are vital. We have taken advantage nearly every year of their 'Summer Centre', when during the school holidays the headquarters are opened up for about a hundred children/adults with the aid of volunteers. A mid-day meal is provided, games and activities, outings, and so on, while the parents have some welcome relief.

But the role of self-help societies does not end here. They have a political role. They began as a lobby to get better services. In the past Mencap and its affiliated local societies have lobbied for better education, more training centre places, more short term care provision, and so on. Now our

127

local Society has a close working relationship with the local authority. Its buildings are used as a Training Centre in the day-time, and in collaboration with the city, the Society has begun to provide homes for short term and longer term care for adults. For much of the membership the spectre of the long-term future is looming large. The Society has also supplied parents with regular information about their rights — in terms of education, allowances, training centre provision, etc. The Society performs a public relations role, participating in community events with floats and stalls. Its float won the Lord Mayor's Show several times. Much of the life of the Society revolves around money-raising, but then that involves people in doing something together, and brings the problems to public attention. A notable recent event was the Walkathon, when thousands walked the twenty-five miles round Birmingham's outer circle route, and the sponsorship money went towards establishing a new home for the Mentally Handicapped. This meant collaboration with BRMB radio, and a good deal of positive publicity. There can be little doubt that the Society has not only enabled many people to cope for many years with the problem of having a handicapped member, but has also contributed to the improvement in facilities and in public attitudes.

Yet there are those who feel they need a more insistent voice. I have come across independent parents' organizations, like Post Help, which concentrate on political lobbying, writing to MPs and Councillors, and pressing the needs upon those in authority. One good thing about our society is that many informal things can happen outside the 'public structures'. A few years ago I was called to a small gathering of parents whose children used the short term care provision at one of the local authority hostels. We were alerted to the lack of provision once our children reached eighteen. Out of that evening came two *ad hoc* meetings with the Chairman of Birmingham's Social Services Committee, local authority officials, parents and social workers all present. There was no formal agenda. We simply got the officials on the line and said, 'What about so-and-so?' and they told us their latest plans. One of the fascinating things was to see how the chance was taken by concerned social workers and harassed parents to bring up individual cases of particular hardship, and how these were taken up by the Councillor. I begin to think that the most positive advances in our society are not made in the glare of publicity, and the bally-hoo of demonstrations, but in the unobtrusive pains-taking work of dedicated local politicians and MPs, making the system work for people; and in the quiet and persistent work of drawing the attention of such people to real needs and hardships.

We are among the lucky ones. We have never had any financial problems. We have had support and help from our families, friends and neighbours. Arthur has for the most part inspired affection from all who have had to deal with him. We were offered a place in a City Nursery to mix him with normal children and aid his development. He was just at the right age at the right time to get a place in a Special School without waiting on a waiting list. He has been on a rota for short term care for some years, and we have had wonderful service from the staff. We have had a comparatively easy time. Circumstances have even brought about a situation which opened up my relationship with his consultant, so that we share our deeper concerns from time to time. What I have been trying to do in this chapter, however, is to use some of the ambiguities in even my comparatively good experience to highlight some of the less encouraging aspects of our society, and to speak for those who cannot speak for themselves. Society may need

PART B
A Way through the Maze?

INTRODUCTION

Since telling the story I have on a number of occasions been asked to contribute to conferences or give lectures on the theological or educational issues raised by the mentally handicapped. The second part of this book attempts to bring together these further thoughts, and so develop the story in a way that approaches theological questions more systematically and less personally. The style should not, however, deceive. The articulation of questions and challenges is far from unrelated to the ongoing daily business of being with Arthur and coping with his physical needs. And the predominant feeling I have now is a sense of not having arrived, despite the assurance of the earlier account. Still we go on in a kind of maze, and there are new joys and new distresses to be experienced, and old ones to go through again. The rough places on the pilgrimage are not all made plain, and the mystery of the 'Skallagrigg' still haunts the mind . . .

What do I mean by the 'Skallagrigg'? Two apparently disconnected things happened about the same time. It took several weeks for the two to come together, and now it is not clear which came first, but so often the notion of coincidence seems utterly inadequate to the oddities of life. One was a conversation that led me to begin thinking about shaping this book. The other was a tutorial with a student who handed me a novel sent on loan by a former student who thought I might be interested. It was William Horwood's *Skallagrigg* (1986, Penguin 1988).

'Skallagrigg', said the blurb on the cover, 'unites Arthur (curious coincidence in itself!), a little boy abandoned many years ago in a grim hospital in northern England, with Esther, a radiantly intelligent young girl who is suffering

from cerebral palsy, and with Daniel, an American com-
puter-games genius. Skallagrigg — whatever the name
signifies, whoever he is — will come to transform all their
lives. And William Horwood's inspired, heart-rending story
of rescue and redemptive love will undoubtedly touch
yours too. . . .'

That evening I began to read. Within half an hour I was
in floods of uncontrollable tears, and I knew that it would
have to wait until after the end of term. So it was that several
weeks later, as I began to put together this larger version of
Face to Face, I tried again, found the novel impossible to put
down, and saw the connection. So it was that this part was
renamed *A Way through the Maze?*

Skallagrigg is a Twentieth Century story, dependent on
the contemporary culture of computer games, on the
discovery that people suffering from cerebral palsy may be
remarkably intelligent, and on the radical change in public
policy with regard to handicapped people. Yet it is also a
story of an oral culture, of the growth of a 'mythology', and
an exploration of the most profound human questions. It
is not an allegory, and yet it is in its way allegorical, the whole
story, together with many of the discrete elements that
make it up, being a parable of the human condition. It
resists simple summary, and in any case would be spoiled if
I revealed the solution — if there be one solution, which I
doubt.

Esther first hears of Arthur and the Skallagrigg from a
spastic friend with whom she alone can communicate.
Then she picks up more and more stories from casual
meetings and contacts. The Skallagrigg appears to be a
kind of 'Saviour' figure in whom Arthur puts his whole trust
and hope, and who from time to time is present with him.
Arthur and his friends are persecuted by Dilke, the Staff
nurse who ruled his Ward for years with an iron hand, and

it is Arthur who communicates the strength and confidence that keeps them going, with promises that the Skallagrigg will come one day. The Skallagrigg is a secret restricted to the sub-culture of a handicapped society, yet spreading inexorably from one to another.

One day as Esther lies helpless in the mud, her wheel-chair having spun over in the wind when her Down's Syndrome friend and helper was not at hand, she realises that Arthur and the Skallagrigg are real, and she embarks on a great research project. By now, though she is helpless and unable to speak, her intelligence has become clear — she communicates through a keyboard and VDU screen, and will eventually get a place at Oxford to read mathematics. With assistance she sets out to trace Arthur's Hospital, to find him and Dilke and the Skallagrigg. Her research takes her into the deeper regions of the stacks under the Radcliffe Camera, to the fast emptying nineteenth century hospitals of Northern England, and eventually to a Professor of Music in Cambridge. Along the way she grows up, and her adolescent problems of 'self' and dawning sexuality are compounded by the impossibility of accepting her physical self. The book explores the faith, hope and love which paradoxically co-exist with boiling anger, with silence, grim darkness and broken relationships, which means there is no room for sentiment. Belief and unbelief emerge as two sides of the same coin.

So Esther's story, Arthur's story, the search for the Skallagrigg, even the story of her father and her grandparents and her lover, parallel one another in their need for redemption, in their moments of utter helplessness, in the strength imparted to one another, even by the weakest to the strongest. There's a dying and rising, a 'networking' of support which transcends distance, a common experience of discovery when the masks are broken down, when selves steeled against facing the darkness of the truth have their false strength broken, when people stop trying to pin the blame for what's happened, and in vulnerability the Skallagrigg is revealed.

But there are no simple answers, and with Daniel's help Esther builds all this into the most original computer game ever devised, in which people face questions about whether people like her should be kept alive, and the player has to find the right option (which seems to be 'Don't know!') in order to go on. . . . So life in all its complexity, its darkness and excitement, is mirrored in complex mazes modelled on the Radcliffe stacks, and at the highest level of the game, in the mighty waves of the ocean that swallowed up her lover's friend leaving him marked for life — until he goes through the horror of the surf with Esther's will to live and succeed. The game's programme is eventually completed through the final wilderness of Esther's withdrawal from being a mother yet not a mother to her infant son. She has to cease to be so that her Skallagrigg can come into being.

The overt religion in the book is the sort of religion we meet in actual churches, sometimes real but often shallow compared with what is left unstated. Almost inadvertently my summary of the story has adopted the language of the Christian story, and at times, the characters seem clad in the *imago Christi*, even if like much else, things are left inexplicit. It reminds me of a moment that occurred some time after I originally wrote the story in *Face to Face*, a moment when Arthur, as it were, bore the stigmata.

I had been invited to share with the Othona community for a week, providing a lecture each afternoon and joining the community in its worship, work and holiday for that period. Some of my family came too, including Arthur. Each morning and evening we gathered for prayers in the oldest place of Christian worship in England still in use, St

Peter's Bradwell, an Anglo-Saxon chapel constructed on the sea wall out of the stones of the old Roman fort of Othona, which had been built to keep the Angles and Saxons out. Members of the community humped Arthur's chair across the fields. Birds flitted around the bare stone chapel, and on the altar was a cross of nails, a reminder of the purpose of the community, founded to work for reconciliation between peoples after the last war. The community is housed in an old army camp.

As usual Arthur could not be kept quiet. So one evening the person leading prayers created 'silence' through the music of the Othona Psalms—and Arthur suddenly seemed to be the Christ among us. The 'Skallagrigg' in the end seems to be each person's *alter ego*, and yet never loses that 'Saviour'-like quality. How that can be is explored in other terms in these papers. For strangely the redeeming Christ becomes the *alter ego* of all humanity, but can only become so when we admit our utter vulnerability, our 'handicap'. The first great Biblical scholar Origen suggested that difficulties and impossibilities were deliberately included in scripture in order to alert us to the fact that its 'surface' meaning is insufficient, and deeper meanings must be teased out. The mystery of the 'Skallagrigg' suggests something similar about the meaning of life: there is no redemption without the cry of God-forsaken-ness.

To write a novel like *Skallagrigg* means entering imaginatively into the world of someone suffering from cerebral palsy, as well as knowing experientially the feelings and reactions of those able-bodied people most closely involved. The author has a daughter with Cerebral Palsy, we are told. Since writing *Face to Face* I have become more acutely aware of the problems of 'projecting' our models onto the handicapped in the vain attempt to make sense of the 'surd', and by doing so, failing to realise the importance of entering their world. But how do we do it? *Skallagrigg* sensitively portrays the slowness, the limitations and the extraordinary love and loyalty of Tom with Down's Syndrome, but the world which comes alive is one where there is intelligence but profound difficulty in communication. This we can identify with, because we share perceptions with it. Far more difficult is to imagine a world in which little sense is made of what is perceived. Once I was given some insight into Arthur's world, and strangely enough what emerges is the same sense of struggling to find a way through a maze which is scary, yet exciting and redeemed by faith, hope and love:

PERCEPTION

Imagine a life with sight but no sense —
A life full of colour and movement and shapes
But no objects or space. Wouldn't it seem
That reality must be a random pretence?
Does blindness mean darkness? Or is it a kind
Of incomprehension that shuts off the mind?

Imagine a life with sound but no word —
A life full of music and buzzing and shouts
But no structure or form. Could meaning be there
At all, or would everything be absurd?
Does deafness mean silence? Or is it a kind
Of incomprehension that shuts off the mind?

But patterns are there, and proportion discerned
In the slatted light of Venetian blinds,
In the fractals of trees or the web of a grill;
And so some sense of beauty is learned.
Yet much blindness remains, and still there's a kind
Of incomprehension that shuts off the mind?

But expressions are there, and moods conveyed
In the tone of voices, in laughter, in tears,

In music's dynamics, its beat and its flow;
So some communication is made.
Yet much deafness remains, and still there's a kind
Of incomprehension that shuts off the mind.

Perception has limits. Our handicapped son
Lives a life full of colour and movement and shapes,
A life full of music and buzzing and shouts,
A life full of love and sharing and fun,
But really perception has hardly begun.
He has such limitations — yet still there's a kind
Of mysterious awareness enlarging the mind.

Perception has limits. Blind spots haunt us all.
The meaning of life is barely disclosed.
Beauty and goodness are dimly discerned,
While truth remains hidden — our vision's too small.
As for loving and sharing, our failures appal.
We have such limitations — but still there's a kind
Of mysterious transcendence enlarging the mind.

Chapter 7

THE DARK SIDE OF LOVE

Telling the story involved theological reflection along the way, and in the Finale of the original I briefly turned to some thoughts on the cross and judgment. At a conference I was asked about this section, and admitted that it needed further thought. For one thing, I now see how easily I slipped from one sense of the word 'judgment' to another. So here I return to the maze, and as in a computer-game travel from one room to another picking up keys along the way. The question is whether they will eventually open all the doors. We will begin in the original room where clearly some tidying up needs doing, but clues suggest that Skallagrigg is lurking near.

Initial explorations

Earlier I indicated a certain dissatisfaction with an entirely cross-centred faith. Christian faith is also about resurrection, whatever that may mean; it is about trust and hope for the future. Yet I still think that the dimension of the cross has to be taken very seriously. There is abroad in the church an unrealistic idealism, an activism which is virtually a triumphalism. It takes both political and charismatic forms: if only we engage in the right activities, the bomb will be banned, oppression cease and the kingdom of God will be established. Not all activism develops into this kind of utopianism, but the danger is always there. I have indicated reservations about the current humanist endeavour to triumph over handicap, suggesting that it arises from the wrong values; I would indicate too reservations about these Christian forms of triumphalism, reservations which I be-

lieve have their roots in scripture. Christian forms of triumphalism also arise from too high a regard for 'success'
values, and too little for the scriptural virtues of humble
acceptance and reliance upon grace. Indeed, my main
reservation concerns the emphasis on human activity: there
are many aspects of life as we now know it about which
human beings can do nothing, and to deny this reality is
fantasy. Because 'science' and modern medicine have given
us longer life, and affluence has brought a more comfortable standard of living, and hospitals have removed death
from the home, we have lost the sense of mortality which
earlier generations felt so strongly. Because of success in
some areas, we have foolishly imagined we can sort the
world out, in spite of all the evidence to the contrary which
forces itself on our attention news bulletin by news bulletin.
There are things we can do nothing about. Certainly handicap and death fall into this category, and I guess sin does
too, which means that visions of a humanly achieved utopia
are fantasy — and they are certainly not biblical. The
appropriate response to the human condition, which is also
the biblical response, is to rely not on our own endeavours
but on the power of God, to open our eyes to a transcendent
dimension and a future possibility beyond our present
condition. Granted the Bible and the story of Jesus is about
God bringing order out of chaos, good out of evil, liberation from slavery, healing from sickness, redemption from
sin, and we are called to participate in this divine activity, to
engage in this dynamic process in the power of the Spirit;
granted the preaching of Jesus calls us to discern the
present reality of God's kingdom and live as though it is
already a reality; the end of the story is still the cross,
submission to apparent defeat, a bearing of the consequences of all that is wrong in the world. There is no escape
from the reality of the cross in this life. The resurrection

transcends this life — it was no magic resuscitation reversing the actuality of a cruel death, but an anticipation of a totally new order of existence, God's new creation.

Now the cross is not only about suffering and affliction, about entering darkness and bearing it, it is also about judgment, and it seems to me we are in danger of losing grip on this aspect of the story. We are uncomfortable about the church's past record of stirring up guilt-feelings, preaching hell-fire, and scaring people into conversion. We make little of God's wrath because we have understood the love of God so simplistically that judgment seems incompatible with it. But judgment is an important element in life whether we like it or not. As long as we are comfortable and successful and everything is lovely, our characters are not tested. It is when things go wrong that we are shown up for what we are, by the way we react, the way we cope. All suffering is a kind of judgment in that it is a crisis (the Greek word *krisis* means judgment) which discriminates in this way. Furthermore you cannot simply divide suffering from judgment. Suffering is quite often our fault — a road accident may be the outcome of a genuine accident like a tyre blown out, or it may be the result of diabolical driving or inadequate maintenance. Cancer or a heart attack may be a desperately sad chance — but increasingly research suggests that habits and lifestyle, diet, smoking, and so on, may well be very important contributors. We do not like the doctrine that suffering is the result of sin because we are all too aware that there is much innocent suffering. But if we approve what Jesus said about the man born blind — that it was not his sin or the sin of his parents which caused him to be born blind — we should also note the story in which he offered the paralytic forgiveness before he healed him. There is a connection between suffering and judgment, between our mistakes, our faults, our habits, and our reaping the consequences of them. Even if we cannot accept this in the case of all suffering of individuals, it is plain that people suffer because people *en masse* behave badly. The bomb is the great scientific achievement of our society, and its judgment.

Handicap is a kind of judgment. Clearly it is not some kind of punishment for sin. It is not usually anyone's fault. Some handicaps are the consequence of careless or blameworthy acts, of course; but the majority arise from sheer accidents or genetic mutations. Some of these mutations may be the fault of a society that allows certain kinds of pollution. But every handicap cannot be explained in such terms of cause and effect. Handicap is not straightforwardly a punishment for sin. But it is a kind of judgment, a *krisis*, because it has that effect. Society, as we have seen, is judged by the way it treats handicapped people, and our society is ambiguous. Many positive things have happened and are happening — attitudes are certainly enlightened compared with the past. There is real concern and genuinely progressive thinking among those concerned with handicap. But for the most part society does not want to know, and the most vulnerable bear the consequences. Handicap discriminates between those who rise to the occasion, and those who fail to do so. It discriminates between the good marriage and the shaky marriage, the stable family and the unstable family. It shows up people and their relationships and their values for what they are. It is a kind of judgment. In the same kind of way, the Gospels, especially the Gospel of John, suggest that people were judged by their reaction to Jesus — they were for or against, they were blind or they saw, their response was a sign of the *krisis* taking place:

> Jesus said, 'For judgment I came into this world, that those who do not see may see, and that those who see may become blind.' Some of the Pharisees near him heard this, and they

143

said to him, 'Are we also blind?' Jesus said to them, 'If you were blind, you would have no guilt; but now that you say, "We see" your guilt remains' (John 9.39-40).

The racist is blind to the sin of his attitude, but the judgment takes place. Those who pass by on the other side and cannot embrace the handicapped, are judged and need redemption. And this redemption is not something we can achieve for ourselves try as we will. It is no good just feeling we ought to be able to respond in a certain way and desperately trying to bury our feelings. It does not work. It takes a miracle of grace for most of us to accept all people as they are. Thus handicap sharpens the judgment and tests our faith. In this life it has to be borne, with all its accompanying distress and pain. There is a sense in which we can 'do' nothing about it. There is no magic wand. But the way we handle it is crucial for the creation of true human values and true human community. It provides a constant living parable of human frailty, but also of its potential transcendence through the grace of God.

On the cross Christ sharpened the judgment, showing up the pride and self-confidence of religious men who thought they were doing God's will in getting rid of him, the compromise of a Pilate who was only doing his job in trying to keep the peace in the most notoriously turbulent province of the Empire, the weakness of friends who turned and ran, betrayed and denied. . . . Here was a *krisis*, a moment of judgment in which people, both individuals and institutions, were shown up for what they really were. Christ sharpened the judgment and bore the consequences.

In the New Testament epistles (e.g. I Peter and Hebrews) suffering is a testing, a discipline, a kind of refinement. Paul at the beginning of Romans suggests that the wrath of God is at work in judging the sins and follies of humanity: they are given up to reap the consequences of their own actions.

144

The creation has been subject to futility, he suggests later. It is only through the groaning and travailing, the submission to judgment, that salvation can come. The early Christians saw their suffering under persecution, and the death of Christ on the cross, as a bearing of the final woes of judgment before the coming of God's kingdom.

Judgment and wrath are deeply written into the biblical material. They are the other side of love's coin. There is no mercy without justice, there is no love without demand and expectation. Love expects loyalty, love sets standards, wants the best *of* the loved one, as well as *for* him or her. Standards mean judgment, measuring up, testing, criticism — these are part of love. If that is true in human relations, how much more in our relationship with God. The religious experience of the saints suggests that the deeper you know God, the more aware you become of a kind of pollution, inadequacy, the more you sense that even the greatest moral achievements of human beings are somehow tainted, ambiguous. 'Take me away, and in the lowest deep, there let me be,' sings Gerontius when he reaches God's presence. 'Woe is me; for I am a man of unclean lips and I dwell among a people of unclean lips,' cried Isaiah. He and his people are caught up together in a kind of pollution. Judgment should not be seen simply in individualistic terms. Live coals purge Isaiah's lips and he is sent out with a message of judgment.

The judgment is upon the whole corporate human mess which we still live in, which we are all still party to. Until humanity is aware of it, abandons its sectional self-righteousness and repents, no ideal of love and peace will solve our problems, and the world will go on reaping the consequences of its sin, or as Paul would put it, tasting the wrath and judgment of God. The love of God is a love which is searing like live coals, for our own good. It is purging and painful, searching out the hidden contamination of sin to which we like to close our eyes. It was the pain of that judgment that Christ bore on the cross. He took it upon himself. That is what atonement is about — the bearing of the pain of judgment in love. The early church understood its suffering and persecution as a sharing in that judgment; the wrath of God was at work in the world finally purging creation so as to bring in the kingdom. It began on the cross; it continued in the church as they submitted to abuse, were informed against in the courts, condemned to work as slaves in the mines, even to die.

The church here today is happily not in that position; yet it has been the persecuted church, the church of the oppressed and the afflicted, which has been the strongest and most true to itself, throughout history. The refinement of judgment is important. We need to ponder the insights of the Bible and abandon optimistic idealism of a liberal humanist kind, learn a deeper repentance, and discover how to follow Christ in taking the judgment upon ourselves on behalf of our society and our world. It is through that refining and discriminating process that we shall find salvation, not through shallow optimism or frantic activism. There is a judgment someone has to bear. Somehow the church should be bearing the judgment; for Paul speaks of 'filling up what is lacking in the sufferings of Christ'. The pain of purging alone can bring salvation.

But that purging and testing is the process whereby the miracle of grace is brought about. In a sense that is what I have lived through and what this book has been about. Through the darkness and the testing I have been given release. I was no better than anyone else at being relaxed with people different from myself. I too valued achievement — to tell you the truth, I still do. But I have discovered that it is no accident that the words grace and gratitude are related words, in the Greek of the New Testament as well as in the English language. In sharing the confession and absolution, the communion and celebration of the handicapped, and of people very different from myself, I have experienced a foretaste of the heavenly banquet. The bread of life is broken on the cross, the tree of life.

Arthur loves trees. One day he smiled up at the trees in the garden, and I saw reality in all its many dimensions, its beauty and its ambiguity, its tragedy and its transcendence:

> He looked up at the trees
> and I followed his gaze
> to behold
> a moving kaleidescope
> of light and shade
> tossed in the breeze
>
> He looked up at the trees
> and I followed his gaze
> to behold
> a knotted rope dangling
> and nails and thorns
> plaited, and keys.
>
> He looked up at the trees
> and I followed his gaze
> to behold
> a still winter skeleton
> an outline sharp
> etched on the skies.
>
> He looked up at the trees
> and I followed his gaze
> to behold
> a sticky bud bursting
> with life, and death
> touched with surprise.

Praise God.

Journeying deeper

The Greek word *krisis* does indeed mean judgment, but its prime meaning is 'discrimination', a 'separating out' or 'deciding between'. From there it means 'judgment', 'sentence' and 'condemnation'. In the Gospel of John these meanings run into one another. So if more than one meaning of 'judgment' figures in what I wrote, it has a precedent! It sometimes seems as if there are not merely confusions but contradictions in John's Gospel. Compare 3. 17-21 with 9.39-40 (quoted above):

> For God sent the Son into the world, not to condemn the world, but that the world might be saved through him. He who believes in him is not condemned; he who does not believe is condemned already, because he has not believed in the name of the only Son of God. And this is the judgment, that the light has come into the world, and men loved darkness rather than light, because their deeds were evil. For everyone who does evil hates the light, and does not come to the light, lest his deeds should be exposed. But he who does what is true comes to the light, that it may be clearly seen that his deeds have been wrought in God.

Here God's purpose in sending his Son is salvation not judgment, there the purpose is stated to be judgment. But here the effect is exposure, and therefore judgment takes place. There is a process of discrimination going on. People's reactions indicate whether they rejoice in the light or hide from it, whether they are blind or can see. Both passages point in the same direction despite their apparent contradiction.

This exposure of true character by reaction to crisis or response to life's trials and tribulations, popular wisdom recognises, and also the fact that it is seen by others, not by the person who is 'judged'. Hence the Pharisees cannot recognise their own blindness because of their confidence that they see. This throws light on the meaning of the saying about the unforgivable sin: what is this sin against the Holy Spirit? Examine the context in Mark 3.21-30. The scribes have just accused Jesus of casting out demons by the power of Beelzebub, the prince of demons. They are so spiritually blind that they mistake the Spirit of God for the spirit of evil. Such blindness cannot be forgiven precisely because they are sure they are right, therefore they will never repent, therefore they cannot receive forgiveness. Forgiveness can only be received if the offender is prepared to climb down. To climb down in this case would mean a radical change in fundamental outlook. As suggested above, the racist is in the same case: proud of his views, not ashamed, unconscious of the judgment that is inevitably taking place.

The attitudes of people and of society to the handicapped effect a similar exposure or judgment. For as I suggested before, handicap has the effect of judging or discriminating between those who rise to the occasion and those who do not, and I would stand by that suggestion, only noting that people's positive reactions are usually very mixed, somewhere between acceptance and non-acceptance, anger and love, sorrow and joy. Given all that, there is a world of difference between ambiguous but positive response and the rejection which thinks only of banishing and denying. There are things in life, of which handicap is one, which discriminate between people, or rather show people up for what they are, expose their true character. By these character is 'tested' or 'proved'.

THE TEST OF THE BEST

Winter snow —	Handicap —
an overflow	the overlap
of white delight,	of light and night,
a bitter blow	a bitter trap

for old and cold,
yet a taste you know
of heaven's leaven.

Winter snow —
a testing blow
judgment starting,
ways parting.
Some entranced,
joy advanced,
hearts excited;
others blighted
by disruption
and destruction.
Children sliding,
sledges gliding,
snowballs hiding.
Weather chiding
parents moaning,
teachings groaning,
Traffic blocked.
Victims shocked.
People glaring,
people staring,
people sharing,
people caring.
Some enraged;
but others freed
new games to lead —
pain and sorrow
death advancing;
life enhancing.

Winter snow —
God's own rod,
the strife of life
in love's fur-glove,
an overflow
of white delight,
or bitter blow

for mother's love,
yet the rising sap
of heaven's leaven.

Handicap —
a testing trap:
judgment starting,
ways parting.
Some attracted,
love exacted,
problems tended;
some offended
by monstrosity,
awful oddity.
Children smiling,
tickling, giggling,
playthings piling.
Cases filing
doctors moaning,
parents groaning.
Language blocked.
Victims mocked.
People glaring,
people staring,
people sharing,
people caring.
Love enraged
by so much need
and more love freed —
fear and sorrow
fun and laughter
life enhancing.

Handicap —
God's own rod,
the strife of life
for mother's love,
the overlap
of light and night,
a bitter trap

is winter snow,	is handicap,
so a taste you know	so the rising sap
of heaven's leaven.	of heaven's leaven.

It was in that poem that these ideas about discrimination began to be honed, especially the parallel between handicap, with all its ambiguity, and other experiences. How to react to snow — is it good or bad, beautiful or deadly, a curse or a blessing? — is just as unclear as how to react to handicap. Yet our reactions show us up for what we are, and the appropriate reaction seems to be a strange mixture of the positive and the negative. This might seem to contrast with the apparently clear discrimination between light and darkness in John's Gospel: yet the story of the blind man is surely one in which the removal of blindness is merely the first step in progress towards understanding and responding appropriately to the challenge of Jesus. 'My hour has not yet come,' Jesus keeps saying, but then 'the hour has come for the Son of man to be glorified', and it is in the dying of a grain of wheat that it bears much fruit: 'Now is the judgment of this world'. The light is in the world, but the glory is veiled until it enters the darkness. There are those who are blind and cannot stand the light, but there are also those who see the signs without believing, and those who see and believe without understanding, and in the end, blessed are those who believe without seeing.

So far we have picked up the following keys:

1. Judgment takes place through response to what we may call 'crisis', events, persons, realities which confront us, and show us up for what we are by our reactions.
2. Like those judged in the parable of the Sheep and the Goats, we are surprised when confronted with this: we had no idea — 'When did we see thee hungry and feed thee?'

151

3. What is condemned and unredeemable is the blindness and hardness of heart which simply cannot respond or see anything good in whatever effects the 'crisis', and so turns its back.
4. What is approved is a range of reactions, more like Skallagrigg's 'Don't know' as the starting-point of the game, yet containing a germ of faith, hope and love, glimpsing glory through a glass darkly.

Taking responsibility

Judge not that ye be not judged: but clearly we are under judgment all the time (though who does that judging has not been specified beyond noting it is not ourselves but others). We cannot avoid being judged and conversely we cannot go through life without making judgments. We must distinguish between good and evil, despite knowledge of good and evil coming from the fruit of the forbidden tree. As parents and teachers we are constantly passing judgment on the work and behaviour of those in our charge, and life consists of assessing other people, their capabilities, their character, their attitudes. We measure and we test.

But when we speak of 'using our judgment' we are usually referring to things where there are no clear rules or precedents to follow. The word 'discrimination' has come to have very negative overtones in our society, usually implying 'discrimination against', suggesting non-acceptance of those who are different, making a sharp distinction between black and white, male and female, etc. But 'to exercise discrimination' is another way of saying 'to use judgment', and as we have seen, that usually suggests that there is no clearly right or wrong action or attitude to take. The root of all these words is 'separation', and verbal usage both alerts to the interconnectedness of these ideas and confuses things for us. Both 'discrimination' and 'judgment' may have good and bad overtones, good and bad consequences. Notice how often the bad side arises from making sharp distinctions, imagining that there is a clear difference between black and white, male and female, right and wrong, good and evil. On the other hand to suppress difference can lead to more subtle forms of unacceptable discrimination, as the reaction against liberal colour-blind responses to racism has clearly shown. Using judgment implies a complexity of appropriate response which cannot be reduced to clear-cut distinctions and predetermined rules.

So the way to the 'Skallagrigg' lies through 'Don't know' as the response to the question, 'Should handicapped people be kept alive?' The dogmatism of the Life organisation comes under judgment, because they outlaw the possibility of 'making judgments' and learning to live with the consequences, because they will not recognise the necessity of taking responsibility rather than falling back on unalterable principles. There is some delicacy in coming to a decision between right and wrong. The problem with lawmaking about abortion is that law cannot allow for delicacy: clear-cut rules determining decisions have to be laid down.

So should we reduce the process of judgment to legal analogies? Is the protest against legalism attributed to Paul bound to burst the legal categories of his thinking? Is this the key (no. 5) to some of the doors that most resist entry, namely that judgment implies a measure of uncertainty and taking responsibility for unclear decisions? As Bonhoeffer put it, the free responsibility of free men 'depends on a God who demands responsible action in a bold venture of faith, and who promises forgiveness and consolation to the man who becomes a sinner in that venture'. On those grounds Bonhoeffer could plot to assassinate Hitler, could dare to sin in order to oppose evil. (Reference: *Letters and Papers from Prison,* Enlarged Edition, ed. Eberhard Bethge, SCM 1967, p. 29).

Meeting with tests

Part of growing up is submitting to judgment, being tested, measuring oneself against others. If neither school nor home provides testing and challenge, the teenager will seek it, in daredevilry, vandalism, peer-group rivalry, or more harmless pursuits like competitive sport. To provide a testing environment is part of loving, of fostering development into maturity, encouraging self-reliance.

PASSION

Step by spiral step, narrow and dark,
Up and up we ascend this Breton spire.
Breathing hard we crawl higher and higher,
Step by step with mounting anticipation
To emerge and be struck by the wind's exhilaration,
Poised on stony lacework tinged with fear,
Whipped by the gale which penetrates the clear
Well-perforated gallery high above
The rooftops of the town. A kind of love,
Terror and joy leaves us dizzy. Yet here
Is where the tension of truth begins to sear
Our minds, as awe leaves its mark.

Wave on curling wave, towering with spray,
Over and over we leap and swim and shout.
Breathing hard we splash and roll about,
Wave by wave with mounting exultation
To float and be lifted by swelling undulation.
Or tossed in the crystalline surf, wildly to leap,
Whipped off our feet by the ocean's suction. Deep
And dark is the power playing push and shove
With helpless flotsam. A kind of love,

Excitement and fear claims energy. Yet strain
Is where the tension of truth begins to pain
Our bodies, as joy has its way.

Mile on struggling mile, windswept and wet,
On and on we pedal and shift our gears,
Breathing hard as each hill-crest appears,
Mile by mile with rising circulation,
To freewheel down the slopes with animation,
Sweeping on scudding wheels around the curves,
Whipped by the elements, living on our nerves,
Weary with painful joints yet determined enough
To keep going on. A kind of love
And adventurousness leaves comfort behind. The pain
Is where the tension of truth begins to claim
Our wills, as searching challenges are set.

Twist by bitter twist life tautens the thread;
But without its tension living would soon be dead.

There is a very strong streak in the Bible which treats
suffering as a testing discipline intended to produce maturity, and there can be no doubt there is truth in this both for
sufferer and comforter, and it marries well with the discrimination idea already explored. Paul speaks of suffering
producing endurance, and endurance character, and
character hope (Romans 5.3-4). The Epistle to the Hebrews
is all about the journey of faith through testing, Jesus
himself learning through suffering and temptation (5.8),
and being the pioneer and perfecter of a faith which could
endure the cross for the joy set before him (12.2). So
picking up the book of Proverbs, the author (12.5-13)
insists on the discipline of God, the need to keep up
courage when punished by the Father, for it is those he
loves that he disciplines, and God is treating those who
suffer like sons: 'For the moment all discipline seems
painful rather than pleasant; later it yields the peaceful fruit

155

of righteousness to those who have been trained by it.'
Judgment, discipline and assessment are part of the process
of love.

But this key only opens some doors. For this whole
approach fails to take seriously the profoundly destructive
effect suffering can have, often damaging quite innocent
victims. Furthermore it encourages our damaging devotion
to success values, producing élitist and discriminatory attitudes to the handicapped. We need judgment to distinguish what appropriate values are.

WHO CARES?

A sparrow	No sparrow
falls to the ground	falls to the ground
with a broken wing.	forgotten by God
What a shame!	who cares.
A youngster	A youngster
crashes his car,	crashes his car;
a wheelchair case:	a testing case
who's to blame?	he shares.
Everyone speaks of tragedy,	Everyone speaks of tragedy,
yet a hidden fascination	yet a hidden fascination
festers in secret jealousy:	enhances popularity:
coddled in bandages,	confined by handicap,
cradled in sympathy,	stifled by circumstance,
loads of attention,	loads of attention
and no expectation:	is given to others.
he's out of the race.	He's out of the race,
He'll be wheeled around	but he's wheeled around
relaxing in luxury,	developing dignity,
basking in sympathy,	loved for discoveries
every achievement	of grace and humour,
a source of wonder,	a matter of wonder,
congratulation	appreciation
without expectation.	beyond expectation.

156

Everyone speaks of tragedy,	Everyone speaks of tragedy,
yet his secret pain and	yet his secret pain and
frustration	frustration
festers in hidden enmity:	polishes hidden sanctity:
confined in fetters	released from pressure
and stifled by pity,	and freed from ambition,
pushed to the margins	pushed to the margins,
and kept in his place,	accepting his place,
he's out of the race.	he's out of the race.
He'll be wheeled around	But he's wheeled around
with his lost independence,	with growing assurance,
lacking in dignity,	taking an interest,
praised for achievements	fostering efforts
of minimum value,	of maximum value,
congratulation	appreciation
without expectation.	beyond expectation.
A youngster	A youngster
crashes his car,	crashes his car,
a wheelchair case,	a wheelchair case,
going through life	going through life
a broken self.	a self matured.
Is it worse than a sparrow	It's more than a sparrow
that falls to the ground?	that falls to the ground,
Does anyone care?	and everyone cares.
Can a self be mended,	For a self is mended
or a broken wing	— a broken wing
give flight from the confines	gives flight from the confines
of this world's love,	of this world's love
a love ambiguous,	to a love transcendent,
hiddenly jealous?	secret, resplendent.

Judgement in love

If having expectations of those we love, submitting them
to judgment (key no. 6), is essential to their development,
then disappointment and anger are part of the loving
process. Like Esther's father we need to be proud of our
children: his redemption comes only at the end of the novel
when he sees Esther anew in her beautiful granddaughter.

157

If we are let down but take no notice, we demean our relationship and declare a lack of love. We have been too long misled by the easy distinction between *agape* and *eros*: Nygren himself recognised that he was describing 'motifs' rather than true linguistic distinctions, a point many of his followers have failed to grasp — but more serious is the disservice it does to any profound appreciation of what love is. Yes, disinterested love even for the unloveable seems an excellent way compared with the possessiveness and selfish jealousy that so often passes for love. But it implies in the end a love that does not care, and therefore is not love. Love passionately desires the best for and the best of the beloved. Love must speak the truth, even if it be in judgment and anger.

For speaking the truth in love may well mean giving vent to anger. Anger is the dark side of love which demands that judgment take place, and without it there is no hope of change, no expectation for the future. Judgment is the reverse side of redemption's coin, because only exposure of the truth can bring the fruits of repentance and the possibility of change: that is why the purpose of the coming of Jesus can be presented both as judgment and as salvation in John's Gospel. Alastair Campbell has already explored *The Gospel of Anger* (SPCK 1986) and there is little point in travelling over the same ground. Suffice it to pass on a few sentences and some of his quotations:

> Human anger occurs most frequently under conditions of need, love and involvement (p. 64, quoting A. Rothenberg).

> Anger directly expressed is a mode of taking the other seriously (p. 64, quoting Beverley Harrison).

> Anger against God shows a trust still in God's goodness, despite the darkness of his face. . . . Anger is the undefeated messenger of hope (p. 78).

... the anger of the oppressed must never be deplored or denied. Like the anger of the religious person against God, it is a sign of hope, of faith that one's fellow human beings can be made to listen (p. 79).

... we must use the power of anger to insist upon a true meeting, where, like the covenant God who will not relinquish his beloved, or like the suffering servant whose honesty brings out the truth in others, we want the other to change, for our sake and for theirs (p. 81).

It seems, then, that the deeper we penetrate into the mystery of God, the less we understand rationally why faith endures. ... There was no answer to Job — but in his angry questioning he met his God (p. 107).

Anger and judgment seen as the dark side of love is something that 'nice' church people have long avoided facing, both within themselves and in God. Conservative evangelicals, on the other hand, finding God's wrath and judgment in the Bible, have retained a lively sense of the need for sin to be judged, and for God's wrath to be propitiated, before mercy and forgiveness can be offered. Meanwhile the atheists' critique of God has exploited the problem of evil and suffering to suggest that if God exists, he must be a sadist, a point easily confirmed by reference to biblical stories of God demanding Isaac as sacrifice, or deliberately subjecting Job to torture — even demanding the death of his Son on the cross. Is God a demon? As Alastair Campbell points out, the dark side of anger is violence and hate, seen both in human beings and in some biblical stories of God's destructive power. If some have feared that God was judging human sin, others have urged humanity to sit in judgment on God. Is that blasphemy? Or is it the anger which is the dark side of love, which hopes for change, which longs to confront God's reality?

All these points turn on the presence of judgment in human relationships. When something happens which breaks up a relationship, how is it to be restored? Let us assume that one party has offended the other, either by a deliberate offence or by a failure to fulfil the obligations of the relationship. A cover-up, a mutual agreement to forget, will do nothing to restore the relationship to its former undisturbed state. It takes neither party seriously. Only the anger and judgment of the offended party, the repentance of the offender, the desire to offer reparation and seek forgiveness, the receiving of that reparation as a token of forgiveness and reconciliation can restore, or rather create anew, the relationship that was broken.

For this process to be possible both offender and offended has to have the imagination to see it from the other person's point of view. If the offender attempts to make excuses for the act, or justify him/herself, then the repentance is not genuine and even if forgiveness were offered, it could not genuinely be received. If the one offended remains angry and anxious to exact penalties, demanding justice and refusing to accept reparation, or simply brushing it all aside, then clearly hope of reconciliation is misplaced. What complicates things even more in human relationships is that there is rarely an innocent party: consider a family feud, for example, or a case of adultery or marriage breakdown. Both may be partly offender, partly offended, and restoration requires that both climb down, both stop justifying themselves and admit responsibility, both accept reparation and offer forgiveness. Seeing one's own responsibility when one feels the victim is desperately hard, but only that can lead to acceptance of any mediating verdict and a positive future.

Atonement implies judgment as the dark side of love (key no. 7). Does it perhaps also imply a two-way process? Does love demand theodicy as another aspect of judgment? Is there a double-lock to which the dark side of love is the key?

AUSCHWITZ AND EVOLUTION

Noughts and a cross on a cosmic scale —
    extinct ova in millions,
    protozoa in billions.
Noughts and a cross — calculations fail.

Noughts and a cross on a human scale —
    families unsung in millions,
    old folk and young in billions.
Noughts and a cross — computers fail.

Noughts and a cross, genocidal the scale —
    gas-chamber dopes in millions,
    prayers and hopes in billions.
Noughts and a cross — all efforts fail.

Noughts and a cross, catholic the scale —
    prisoners hounded in millions,
    tortured and wounded in billions.
Noughts and a cross — must martyrs fail?

Noughts and a cross on a bestial scale —
    refugee hordes in millions,
    sick, starving herds in billions.
Noughts and a cross — when sympathies fail.

Noughts and a cross on a prodigal scale —
    damaged foetuses — millions,
    rotting carcasses — billions.
Noughts and a cross — life's creatures fail.

Noughts and a cross, universal the scale —
    light years and stars in millions,
    genes, germs and scars in billions.
Noughts and a cross — conceptions fail.

161

Is it nothing to you,
you god of this world,
failed demiurge?

It is all to me, Job.
For mine is the game —
I reckon each nought
and the cross is my shame.
It's me who's the purge,
it's me who's the surge
of creation's great loss
by noughts and a cross.

Judgement and Atonement

The trouble with judgment is that it so easily gets trapped in the law-courts, since it always seems to imply that analogy. So there is a moral code (the Law) which the party in the dock is accused of breaking. The rules mean it is all clear-cut: either he/she did or did not do it. If guilty, then the sentence is condemnation and punishment must ensue.

There is civil justice, which regularises relationships between citizens, involving property, marriage, contracts, etc. This is a way of objectifying the kind of breakdown in personal relationships discussed above, submitting it to outside adjudication, assigning blame, exacting reparation, re-establishing the status quo. Clearly it is possible for someone else to act on behalf of the person sentenced by paying the penalty without undermining the process of justice (e.g. a parent paying a fine on behalf of a juvenile).

There is also criminal justice. This is not simply a matter of personal relationships. The punishment of crime is undertaken by the state. The justification of punishment may be in terms of deterrence, retribution or reformation. Whichever it is (and the point is much debated), the punishment has to be meted out to the criminal: to punish a substitute would universally be regarded as unjust. Justice demands that the criminal himself get his deserts.

Clearly the idea of God as Judge is deeply rooted in the biblical material, and the imagery of the Last Great Assize has had a long life from the writings of St Paul down the centuries. Sin is a bit like crime, and sins like broken laws. Yet despite the long tradition of using keys drawn from the legal analogy, we may well find on reflection that they do not fit the locks sufficiently exactly. The so-called 'penal substitution' theory confuses civil and criminal law, and tries to force the complexity of reconciliation into a legalistic model which provides an unjust outcome. Maybe God has to use his judgment in dealing with his wayward children.

But to turn to the other traditional accounts of atonement is no more satisfactory. The view that God simply demonstrated his love and forgiveness on the cross, and this effects a response of repentance, misses the structures of obligation in relationships, the element of anger and discipline which inevitably belongs to love. The idea that Christ overcame the powers of evil on the cross projects evil onto a usurping 'god' or 'devil', so failing to accord responsibility to the parties in the relationship, allowing human beings to regard themselves as victims rather than sinners, allowing God off the hook when it comes to all the 'gonewrongness' of his creation, and again ignoring the importance of judgment. We cannot abandon the notion of judgment even if we find the law-court analogy insufficient.

Suppose there is a kind of double reparation made on the cross. On the one hand, as I suggested long ago in *Sacrifice and the Death of Christ*, God takes responsibility for the mess we protest against, offering reparation for creating a world like this, giving up his only-begotten Son to suffer the consequences of all the 'gonewrongness' of

163

which we accuse him, the suffering and the sin, the pain and purposeless devastation — for all of which he admits responsibility. On the other hand, the man Jesus by his complete sacrifice of obedience unto death, offers reparation on our behalf, pays our fine as it were, and invites us to take advantage of this, to receive the amnesty God offers, the overlooking of past sin that righteousness may be effected in us through the new covenant written in our hearts. . . .

For this attempt to restore relationships, the structures of obligation have to be met, the responsibility of each party respected, judgment and anger have to be expressed and acknowledged for change to be possible. The cross acts as judgment, exposing the sins of those who put Christ to death, and the anger of God against sin which Jesus has to brave and bear on our behalf.

I guess we have picked up enough keys to open a number of doors, but we have not made much progress beyond the room where we started, and as yet have little grasp of the plan of the maze. We still seem to be focussing onto the cross several different meanings of 'judgment', though perhaps now we perceive a certain interconnectedness anyway. But we are hardly ready yet for the higher levels of the game. For one thing, we are speaking of God in dangerously anthropomorphic terms, attributing to him very human passions and reactions, subjecting him to his creatures, who are free to hurt and taunt. Much modern theology has not been afraid to reduce God to this level, but it cannot be done lightly, and in the final chapter we will return to this theme. And another thing closely connected with that point: surely the partners in this process of reconciliation cannot be regarded as equals, and we cannot simply project human experience onto our relationship with God. What about our creatureliness? What about human sin? Should we not take even more seriously the possibility that God's love is a refining fire, that the need for purging goes far deeper than we can imagine? The next chapters will bear on these questions.

Chapter 8

THE DARK SIDE OF HUMANITY

In 1987 I was invited to deliver the Keswick Hall Lecture at the University of East Anglia. When the College of Education was incorporated into the University, the Keswick Hall charity was set up, to sponsor an annual lecture on some aspect of the Christian religion or of religious education. I was asked to speak on a theme arising from my book *Face to Face.* My title was *The Crooked Timber of Humanity — the challenge of the handicapped.*

The posters went up, and naturally enough the quotation I had chosen as my title, appearing out of context and in association with the subtitle, was misunderstood. Just as I was about to prepare the lecture, in which I intended to tackle the problem of social acceptance of the handicapped, I received a protest letter which caused me profound upset, anger that anyone could think a parent should mean what they thought I meant, embarrassment at my own failure to see how it might be read. In the event, however, it sharpened up the whole argument, since it provided a raw example of exactly the issue I was trying to address. The text of that lecture constitutes the content of this chapter. It follows on from the last chapter in that it explores the way in which responses to the handicapped show up the crookedness of human nature, the 'original sin' which brings us under judgment.

The Keswick Hall lecture is supposed to be about some aspect of the Christian religion or of religious education. My subject fits neither perfectly, but both to some degree. It is about education in so far as part of my subject concerns the way society responds to the existence of handicap in its midst, and this could have consequences for our educational and care policies; it is about the Christian religion in so far as I offer theological reflection on our response to the handicapped, and what it reveals about human nature.

Which statement should make clear that the controversial image in my title is not in the first place a reference to the handicapped, still less a derogatory characterisation of them, as I gather some have supposed.

What then was the source and intention of the title? The phrase comes from the philosopher Kant. The full sentence reads: 'Out of the crooked timber of humanity can nothing straight be made'. Clearly he meant, as I mean, the whole of humanity. Humanity is twisted, or to use the terminology of Christian theology, humanity suffers from 'original sin'. Now I am not a Kantian scholar and I have no idea of the context of the sentence — in any case, I am not now interested in exploring exactly what Kant meant. My use of Kant's words is an example of the fact that meaning is not necessarily confined to the author's original intention. Statements can take on a life of their own. This statement took on a life of its own in my imagination, and came to signify in its ambiguity a whole range of creative associations and meanings which will gradually unfold as we proceed. Unfortunately, it acquired yet further meanings in the minds of some who saw the phrase on posters abstracted from the full quotation.

Now why did the phrase signify for some something derogatory or insulting? It did so because those who responded in that way expected it to. Why did they expect it to? Precisely because they have experienced that reaction all too often and they are defensive. Why have they experienced this? Because humanity is incapable of accepting the handicapped in a natural way — there is something twisted in human response to the handicapped. And that is the point I wish to explore in the first instance, even though that aspect of the matter presumably never entered Kant's head. Most parents have some tale to tell of rejection or prejudice, ostracism or audible remarks that hurt, like the couple I once knew who couldn't bear to take the family on holiday because if they sat on the beach they could feel everyone staring. It's the little things that hurt most, and not least because it is difficult to cope with one's own embarrassment. I vividly remember the first time we pushed our son out in a wheelchair. As long as it was a pushchair, it was OK, I suppose because I could kid myself things were normal. For us now a wheelchair is as normal a part of life as the nappies we have been handling for nearly twenty years. But that first time was a moment of truth, a stage in admitting the reality of abnormality for us as parents and for our family. The interplay of our own ambiguous feelings and the public reactions of others makes us defensive.

A few years ago there was a public scandal about the attitudes of people in Teignmouth. Those who earned their living in the tourist trade, the hotel keepers, the shopkeepers, the Chamber of Commerce, etc., protested about the numbers of mentally handicapped people coming to Teignmouth on holiday, or for day outings. Why? I don't suppose I have to spell it out. We all know why. We may feel scandalised, and there was a press uproar. We may feel people should know better. We may wish to get involved in public education and the effort to change attitudes. But there is an intractable deep-seated problem which society never quite manages to resolve. We may like to think the Church is different. Indeed my experience does suggest that Christian people often respond more positively than other groups in society. But the fact is that my most hurtful experience came from my local Church, and it arose precisely because the handicapped do not fit easily into, dare I say it, 'normal' church life.

And that is the point. On the whole, humanity cannot be natural about the handicapped because — let's be honest if a little blunt — they don't fit. Decent people don't like to have this pointed out. In fact decent people over-compensate, and their reactions are therefore just as unnatural as the negative reactions. Let's face the truth, because only the truth will set us free. It's no good being sentimental about it. Handicapped people trigger gut-reactions in people, and all too often these gut-reactions are negative and destructive. There was a time when I felt very aggressive about this, and rather belligerently determined that we should live as normal a life as possible and other people would have to accept Arthur. But the realities of handicap increasingly prevented this. You cannot force integration. Nor can you simply condemn those people who cannot cope with their own feelings. There was a time when I myself found it profoundly distressing to go to functions at my own son's school — it just highlighted the realities and deepened the pain. Instead of pretending things are otherwise, let us consider why this is the way things are, and what might be done about it.

Part of the problem is certainly fear — fear of the unknown — and hence the importance of public education. Acceptance can only follow understanding. The handicapped are not the only people in our society who suffer in this way. Foreigners have problems — the English are well advised not to retire to that idyllic Welsh village for social reasons! Foreigners who look different have even more problems, and the children of immigrants who are no longer foreigners but have black skins, inherit the stigmas arising from such fears. Our difficulties with accommodating the handicapped have the same roots as racism. It is because people are like us but different that we find it so hard simply to be natural. But there are also those indefinable fears that arise in people when they see someone blind or in a wheelchair — that vague unadmitted fear that it might be me — because the handicapped person is too like us for comfort. Do we stare or do we look away? It is like the horrified fascination that draws crowds to the scene of an accident.

I want to suggest that the work of the anthropologist Mary Douglas may be able to help us understand why as human beings we react in the way we do — though as I expound her theory, I hope you will not jump to conclusions too soon about its application to our problem. I refer to her book, *Purity and Danger* (London 1966). She was concerned to explore and understand religious regulations which seem to us quite irrational, like the distinction between clean and unclean foods in the book of Leviticus, or the various taboos which operate in most primitive societies. She begins her discussion by pointing out that every society has its 'purity' regulations, and they are not necessarily religious. Purity implies the removal of dirt. But what is dirt? Dirt is relative. It is quite simply 'matter out of place'. Food is not dirty in itself, but it is dirty to leave cooking utensils in the bedroom, or food bespattered on clothing. Dirt implies a 'set of ordered relations and contravention of that order. Dirt is never a unique isolated event. Where there is dirt there is system. Dirt is the by-product of a systematic ordering and classification of matter, in so far as ordering involves rejecting inappropriate elements' (p. 35). Our apprehension of the world involves the development of a culture which organises our perceptions, classifies and labels, and as individuals we are educated into the culture of the social group to which we belong. 'Culture, in the sense of the public, standardised values of a community, mediates the experience of individuals. It provides in advance some basic categories, a positive pattern in which ideas and values are tidily ordered' (p. 38).

But 'any given system of classification must give rise to anomalies, and any given culture must confront events which seem to defy its assumptions'. Later in the book, Mary Douglas explains Leviticus' definition of clean and unclean creatures in these terms: the basic distinction for a pastoral herding people is between domestic and wild animals; the problems arise with 'anomalies', those creatures which for one reason or another do not exactly fit the definitions. The important question for any social group is how it makes room for the anomalies or the ambiguities. Anomalies and ambiguities are not, of course, exactly the same, as Mary Douglas admits; but they function for her theory in remarkably similar ways, and she gives examples of things which might be described by either term, because they do not fit predetermined categories. To return to the main point — the question is how a society copes with anomalies and ambiguities. The desire for purity may lead to expulsion, but that kind of purity proves to be 'hard and dead'; 'purity is the enemy of change' (p. 162). Ambiguity may produce laughter, revulsion or shock at different points and intensities, but it is also creative: the margins, the things that don't fit. So in primitive religions, it is not uncommon to find that one or other of the anomalies, a thing that is taboo, becomes in religious ritual the very thing that can produce cleansing and new life (p. 163ff).

Mary Douglas notes the pertinence of this to the way European societies, including our own, have responded to the anomaly of the Jews. 'Belief in their sinister but indefinable advantages in commerce justifies discrimination against them — whereas their real offence is always to have been outside the formal structure of Christianity.' In other words

171

their problem has always been that they do not fit. She might have extended the observation to the whole area of racist attitudes in our society. People exclude whatever does not fit with their assumptions about how the world is. It is hardly surprising that a good deal of her book is concerned with sex taboos: in every human society the distinction between male and female has been an area of ambiguity, and there is much greater public awareness of this problem since she wrote in 1966, as the feminist movement has forced society to face these ambiguities.

But the illumination of her study lies in the fact that it is through the creative handling of anomalies and ambiguities that there is hope for change and new life, not by their systematic exclusion. If you have completely rigid sex taboos, the inevitable result is quite literally barrenness. You have to have contexts in which the taboos do not operate. In primitive societies, religious ritual could 'sacralise' what was normally regarded as taboo: the most taboo area of all, the pollution of death, could be treated in a positive creative way, above all by its ritual acceptance by a willing victim in sacrifice. You don't cope with the anomaly of death by denying its reality, but by facing it in such a way that it becomes life-giving. We need an equivalent to such rituals to allow the anomalous to have a creative role in our society. The desire to exclude may be an inevitable reaction, but it is not the effective answer. The desire to deny that any anomaly exists may be the other way out, but that is a delusion. Somehow the reality of difference must be accepted so that something new and creative can emerge. Supporters and opponents of apartheid, please note.

Against that background let us turn to the handicapped. History as well as anthropology shows that human societies have reacted in various ways to the handicapped, and those reactions indicate the gut-feeling we all have that they are

anomalous and they do not fit. The big institutions carefully placed outside our major cities, though now overtaken
by urban expansion, are vivid reminders of a social policy
that dealt with the anomaly by exclusion. It was a policy that
could be given whitewashing moral rationalisations, but
really reflected the way people felt, including often those
who were the parents of the handicapped person. It is still
the case that in their immediate distress, some parents
cannot cope and reject the child. Others agonise — this
child is flesh of my flesh and bone of my bone, but. . . . Why
me? I used to find it disturbing that all parents I ever met
had awful stories to tell about how they first got to know
about their child's handicap, and few can handle it naturally. But I now recognise that a bad experience of being
told is inevitable. The news is just too traumatic. The
bringer of such news is bound to be blamed no matter how
sensitively it has been handled.

If rejection is not the response, then explanation must be
found. How can I make sense of what has happened? One
way is to settle for an interpretation which reduces or denies
the ambiguity. The letter of protest which I received said,
'May I point out that they are not 'Crooked Timber' but
PEOPLE'. Of course I applaud this healthy reaction against
those past attitudes which dealt with the problem by exclusion. But insisting that there is no difference between the
handicapped and the rest of us, the dogmatic pursuit of
policies of normalisation, is just as unsatisfactory, and may
be equally hurtful.

Almost exactly a year ago, the Pastoral Studies section of
our Theology Department took the issue of the Mentally
Handicapped as the theme of its Spring Conference. We
were discussing 'personhood' and the way in which our
definitions of what a person is, are so often elitist and
exclusive; how the Judaeo-Christian idea of a human being

having been created in the image of God has so often led to a view of humanity which excludes the mentally handicapped. The Chaplain of the local hospital for the mentally handicapped spoke of the real personhood of each one with whom he had to deal, even the most severely limited. Even if there seemed to be no response, you went on in hope, believing that here was one made in the image of God. Question and discussion time followed. Suddenly there was a dramatic outburst — a woman crying out and hammering her fists on the desk in her anger and distress. Our idealistic talk simply did not fit with the reality of her experience. She had to name the horrific reality. Her son was not a human person in any sense that she could conceive. There was no hope because he had a deteriorating condition. You cannot make something the case simply by asserting that it is so.

Mary Douglas gives an example from another culture of how ambiguity may be reduced by interpretation. We may not like the language in which it is expressed, still less the action described, but I don't think we dare avoid it. I quote '. . . when a monstrous birth occurs, the defining lines between humans and animals may be threatened. If a monstrous birth can be labelled an event of a peculiar kind the categories can be restored. So the Nuer treat monstrous births as baby hippopotamuses, accidentally born to humans, and with this labelling, the appropriate action is clear. They gently lay them in the river where they belong. . . .' Redefining is one way of justifying exclusion. It is also a way of pretending the reality does not exist.

Refusal to face the reality is characteristic of so-called enlightened attitudes in our society, and our educational and social policies reflect that process of denial. The prevailing philosophy is 'normalisation'. The handicapped are to be integrated as far as possible with normal life. As far as possible they should attend normal schools, and 'community care' should be the aim of all public policies. Now let me not be misunderstood. For many of the handicapped I have no doubt that this is a good policy, and they are enabled to live far more fulfilling lives than ever they were when they were institutionalised. Furthermore, I have no doubt that the public is gradually being educated to accept and affirm the handicapped in their midst.

But let us not be blind to reality. We sometimes put the handicapped into a situation of grave risk by pretending that they are no different. Parents are usually the people most acutely aware of this. The handicapped are often innocent, trusting and very vulnerable. Our society is often cruel and violent. I shall never forget reading in the magazine *Parents' Voice* an account of an enlightened community home for a small group of Mentally Handicapped people established in an area of new development. The local kids began with harassment in the streets and ended by obtaining access to the home and burning it down. Nor shall I forget the article contributed to the same magazine by a parent whose daughter had been very happy in a 'campus' hospital where she could wander round at will and had many friends and acquaintances, but community care policies meant the closure of the hospital and her discharge into a home where her life would inevitably be more restricted, since she could never be allowed to go out on her own into the dangerous environment of a modern city. Nor shall I forget being told about a chap who lived in a village where everyone knew him, and if they happened to see his flies undone, they just gave him a gentle reminder, then there was a building programme, strangers came, they called the police and the chap was arrested for indecent exposure. What is community care where there is no community?

175

To return to Mary Douglas: marginal people are those 'who are somehow left out in the patterning of society, who are placeless. . . . Their status is indefinable. . . . It seems that if a person has no place in the social system and is therefore a marginal being, all precaution against danger must come from others. He cannot help his abnormal situation.' She goes on to describe how ex-prisoners get stigmatised, often through no fault of their own — society cannot let them live down the past. Society puts labels on people who do not fit, whether we like it or not. Someone in my hearing recently suggested that we shouldn't use the word 'handicapped'; we should speak of people with special needs. OK. Re-label. Substitute Down's Syndrome for mongolism and take away the stigma. But be warned. It's happened before. It will inevitably happen again. Simpleton, imbecile, retarded — none of them were derogatory originally; their basic meanings are quite neutral. In the end whatever term we use will be misused by someone, and it will become derogatory. It is no solution to pretend there is no problem. There is this intractable 'crookedness' in humanity, and you cannot make it straight simply by re-definition. It may be more painful to face the truth, to name the anomaly, but only by doing so, by being honest about the reality, can we turn it into something creative. The taboo subject can be dealt with only if we dare to define it.

Once we have defined it, how can we 'sacralise' it? 'The special kind of treatment which some religions accord to anomalies and abominations to make them powerful for good', said Mary Douglas, 'is like turning weeds and lawn cuttings into compost'. What you throw away becomes manure, contributing to new life. Primitive societies, indeed the people of the Old Testament, took the taboo substance blood and turned it into a means of purification, a symbol not of death but life. What was involved was a shift

176

in perspective as the taboo subject was handled and faced and put into another context. I would suggest that tragedy has always fulfilled a similar function, and it is no accident that it arose in a religious context in classical Athens, and Aristotle spoke of its effects in terms of *katharsis* — purification. Great tragic drama enables us to face up to realities about the human condition that we would rather forget or deny. What we need in relation to the handicapped is a 'conversion-experience', a re-orientation which can face and accommodate the challenge that the handicapped present, whether we like it or not, to our ideology of what is human.

To sum up what I have said so far, and to move us on to the next stage, let me shift the tempo and the rhythm of my discourse. Mary Douglas suggested that ambiguity can be creative, and that the language of poetry exploits ambiguity. Maybe it is only through poetry or drama that we can acceptably speak of what is taboo:

> Eyes averted arrested light on a log.
> Crooked and twisted the fallen timber lies
> Writhing, rotten, no earthly use, the surprise
> Product of blind-folded nature's ill-fitting cog.
> Misted eyelids penetrate heaven's fog.
> Transfigured the antique beauty quite belies
> The usefulness of use. Perfection's prize
> Is seasoned suffering smiling over the bog.
> Flawed from the start, the back grew twisted and bent,
> Yet crooked the smile arrests the averted gaze.
> What was meant to be was surely meant.
> There's more than meets the eye in the morning haze.
> The crooked timber of humanity
> May find in crookedness its sanity.

Yes, I have shifted the application of my ambiguous image, and I do this at the risk of the protesters saying 'I told you so'. But it is not to devalue but to facilitate that shift in perspective which I have suggested is necessary. I love walking in woods, and I find that trees are a constant source of inspiration.

So does my son Arthur. The first word he ever tried to say — and we are still at the stage of poor imitation of sounds rather than conversation — was 'eesh', trees, and he spends hours looking up at their profiles moving in the breeze. For the two of us trees have become symbols of life and death and all things meaningful. The Jewish philosopher Buber in his famous book *I and Thou* actually takes a tree as his example of how people treat what is other than themselves. Mostly we treat a tree as an 'It', an object, something we can exploit, or study as a scientist, or even destroy. Buber noted how often we treat another person as an 'It' rather than a 'Thou'. I guess he would approve Kant's more famous statement: 'Act in such a way that you always treat humanity . . . never simply as a means, but always at the same time as an end.' Now for Buber it was possible to treat even a tree as a 'Thou', to treat it as one would treat a person, with respect, the kind of respect that can receive and not just use or take from, not as a 'means' but as an end in itself. There may be some handicapped people who are so severely limited it is impossible to describe them as persons, but it is never impossible to relate to them as Buber would have us relate to everything in creation.

During the past year I have watched Arthur become more and more physically crooked. It has been painful to acknowledge what is happening, but that's the way it is, and that is why the 'double meaning' of my title is of particular personal significance. The crooked old log in the wood, lying there apparently useless, may be the most picturesque and beautiful thing around. The shift in perspective means recognising that our ideals of what 'perfect' human beings are, are false and mixed up. They are utilitarian and success-oriented. The handicapped often show us what true beauty and true humanity is. Our negative responses arise from the distortion of values that cannot see this. If we can let the handicapped challenge our values, something truly creative can happen which can happen in no other way. In Mary Douglas' terms, what we instinctively wanted to remove or deny, becomes the very thing which brings change, new life, new attitudes.

The key, it seems to me, is establishing a reciprocal relationship with the handicapped. The most fundamental aspect of this is the recognition, not that we are doing them good, but that they are doing something for us. The thing that finally resolved my distress was the discovery that I had to give thanks for Arthur. It was no longer a case of accepting him, but rejoicing in him and receiving from him. I come in bruised and battered from the trials and tribulations of the world, the pressures of University cuts and problem students, and awful committees and people needing me and making demands on me, and there is Arthur to be fed and changed, bathed and lifted, put to bed and got up, in an endless and sometimes wearisome routine — but that is not the whole story. Where I minister to others, Arthur ministers to me. He shows me what life is about, brings me down to basics, gives me peace, helps me to resolve the tensions, and it is with him that I find the fruits of the Spirit: love, joy, peace, patience, kindness, goodness, faithfulness, humility and self-control. Let me not be sentimental or pretend life with Arthur is easy. Sometimes it is frustrating, when he is difficult and uncooperative and won't eat. . . . Sometimes it is distressing, when he cries and cries and can't tell you what's wrong, or when you have to take him to the hospital and watch while doctor or dentist causes him pain. . . . But I know that he has given me so

179

much, and I have been redeemed from a good deal of crookedness by his crookedness.

> Contemplation gazes in the eyes
> Of Nature's accident, a malformed child.
> How can this monstrous sadness still be styled
> Human? This surely must epitomise
> Those awful questions that defy the wise.
> 'Look', some say, by sentiment beguiled,
> 'The soul peeps out'. Absentedly it smiled,
> No eye contact, inert — and vain hope dies.
> And yet this passive form cries out in pain,
> Hungers for basic needs and pants for breath.
> Humanity lies there: we're all the same —
> Vulnerable and frail, defying death.
> Helplessness the image of God reveals.
> Like salt rubbed in the wound, affliction heals.

Nor am I alone in this experience, and you don't need to be a parent for this to happen to you. Last year a couple of our students went on holiday with Arthur and the local Catholic Handicapped Children's Society. Technically they went as helpers. They came back exhausted, but euphoric. It had quite literally been a conversion-experience in which they had come to a quite new appreciation of what life was all about. Those who live and work in the L'Arche communities founded by Jean Vanier could give similar testimonies. It is because they have had this experience that those who help with the local Gateway clubs were so incensed by my title. If we are to be truly human, we need to overcome our fears and our embarrassment and relate to the handicapped, embracing the reality not some whitewashing euphemism. This is the way of redemption from the crookedness explored earlier in this lecture.

Redemption is of course a term from Christian theology. In Christian understanding we find the same sort of dynamics at work. The cross of Christ shows up the reality of human sin, the crookedness which so often leads to the suffering of the innocent, the banishment and destruction of what is good, the mobilisation of the political and religious structures to eliminate change or challenge. Christ was thrust 'outside the camp', banished like the scapegoat, destroyed so that purity could be maintained. He was just too dangerous to be contained. We are all implicated in the shame of it. We and all human societies are judged by that event. It shows us up for what we are. And yet the cross is also the way of redemption. The things we fear, the taboos of blood and death, the curse of the most cruel and despicable punishment humanity has invented, these are all 'sacralised', put in a positive context in which they can be faced and not merely neutralised but overcome. Not for nothing did the mediaeval hymn sing, 'O felix culpa' — O fortunate fault — as the crookedness of sin was transfigured in the crookedness of the cross. Christians have always tended to put roses on the cross, and be sentimental about it, but it will not be effective for our redemption unless we name its horror and shame, unless we receive our redemption through embracing the horror rather than trying to achieve redemption for ourselves by pretending we're not really that bad. We are justified not by our good works or our own efforts, but by God's grace received in faith, by Christ's acceptance of our curse.

In a similar way the handicapped show us up for what we are: crooked and unnatural in our response, unable to accommodate what does not fit with our assumptions and ideals about what a perfect human person is. The horrific ways in which the handicapped are sometimes treated is the tip of an iceberg of human embarrassment. The handicapped present an uncomfortable challenge to the illusion of human greatness, perfection and progress. We used to

181

banish them from our sight in remote institutions, rather as primitive societies designated unclean the things they could not understand. Now we try to make them fit, we set out to 'normalise'. Isn't this a way of trying to make them conform to our success norms? Couldn't behaviour modification be as inhuman as indoctrination, but justified because it makes the victims socially acceptable? So-called enlightened policies are perhaps as problematic as the old banishment. The handicapped, like the cross, reveal us for what we are. Humanity is crooked.

But the handicapped may bring us our redemption. They can effect in us a change of heart, a new set of values, a new perspective. They can show us what true humanity is. There is a sense in which we are all handicapped, we are all mortal and vulnerable, and far from perfect. We need to let the reality of handicap be a critique of our illusions, our ambitions, our much-vaunted achievements. But we also need to let them help us, and not just help them in a patronising way. We need to receive from them, to learn simply to 'be' not forcing them to conform to what we regard as socially acceptable, but adapting our lives and ourselves to involve them in the way they want to be involved — let them make the running for once.

Now unfortunately this is not something about which one can legislate, nor is it something that can simply be produced by public education. History has seen many attempts to bring in the kingdom of God by law or persuasion, but it doesn't work. You cannot force acceptance, and you cannot work miracles by moral exhortation. The fears and responses which produce rejection are unfortunately all too real. Social policies which don't recognise this put the handicapped at risk. Even integrated education is problematic, since we all know that so-called innocent children are little horrors and every school has its bullies:

the bullies are attracted immediately to any who become easy victims — the weak, the disadvantaged, the different — no matter in what way they are different. The difficulties in the way of integrating the handicapped into so-called 'normal' life shouldn't be minimised: my son loves music, but no way could I ever take him to a public concert — his behaviour would not be socially acceptable. At times I expect Church congregations to put up with this, and on the whole they do. But no-one should imagine it is easy. Yet there can be no doubt that those who do not have the experience of relating to the handicapped have missed one of the most beautiful and transforming experiences of life. It's not the handicapped who need community care. It's US. To learn from the handicapped requires a new heart and a new spirit within us, but if we are prepared to learn, it will produce the new heart and new spirit and we will be immensely enriched — indeed, it will be our salvation. We shall discover what it really means to be human.

> Crooked with knots the fallen timber lies.
> Exposed to the elements, draped in decaying moss,
> Its twisted shape begins to resemble a cross.
> Unseen the artist takes the stuff of sighs
> And fashioning the faulted timber tries
> Creation out of uselessness. By loss
> Comes compensation. Tragedies emboss
> The tortured tree of knowledge where death dies.
> Healed by his wounds, we find in paradox
> Our holiness. Taboo's taboo no more.
> Purity's prison-bars pure love unlocks.
> Incurable the sickness finds a cure.
> The crooked timber of humanity
> Has found in crookedness its sanity.

Chapter 9

MADE IN THE IMAGE OF GOD?

In 1986 the Pastoral Studies Spring Conference at Birmingham University focussed on *Mental Handicap, Theology and Pastoral Care*. The question which most clearly emerged concerned the nature of personhood, of humanity, and how it is that the mentally handicapped are to be embraced in our definitions or doctrines of human nature. Rex Ambler contributed a paper on 'What is a person?' and I tried to relate the questions raised by the mentally handicapped to traditional Christian anthropologies. Others spoke of worship with the mentally handicapped, and their membership of churches, and these issues revolved around the same fundamental questions, since how mentally handicapped people are treated clearly relates to assumptions about what they are.

Perhaps most intriguing was a paper by Ian Cohen suggesting that the handicapped are like the *gerim* in the Hebrew Bible, the sojourners or resident aliens, who are part of society and yet cannot be integrated into it: in recognising their difference we need to accept and protect them as Israelite law protected dependent aliens. To treat them as the poor or marginalised assumes the possibility of removing their disadvantage; but in the case of the disabled, that difference is irremovable, and must be dealt with in accordance with that reality. It was another way of grappling with the issue raised in the last chapter.

But the association of the disabled with the *ger* led to deeper possibilities: for the *ger* was to be treated well simply because he represented the true soul of the Israelite, once sojourner in the land of Egypt. A number of the prophets had to live like the *ger*, notably Jeremiah in his lamentations and sufferings. And when we turn to early Christian documents, we find self-identification with the *paroikos*, the Greek equivalent of *ger*, for Christians are citizens of heaven, scattered around the earth as 'sojourners' in a diaspora. So the people of God are *gerim*, and God is protector of the *gerim*. Cohen went so far as to suggest that God himself could be regarded as *ger*, both in the Old Testament and in the New Testament depiction of Christ.

As the novel *Skallagrigg* so tellingly portrays, the able-bodied are 'strangers' in the community of the handicapped, just as the handicapped are 'sojourners' in able-bodied society. Cohen suggests that as love between Israelite and *ger* springs from a shared 'soul', so love between able-bodied and the disabled cannot be based on our need for someone to help. We have to pass over into the 'foreign land' in which they dwell, and find something of our identify there, though there we will always be 'resident aliens'. And as God identifies with the 'sojourner', so Cohen provokes us to ask whether God is disabled, whether there is 'something defective in God which allowed him to be forgiven his failure to protect adequately and always be worthy of dependence'. Community depends on that 'shared soul' which is a 'shared awareness of forgiveness both for God and from God, both for each other and from each other'. Then 'just as the true born Israelite and *ger* could worship God together in their unending dissimilarity, so can those able and disabled today'.

Cohen's paper reinforced the direction of my own thoughts, the feeling that my wrestling with the 'meaning' of mental handicap had been focussed too much on the problems able-minded people have. The justification of handicap that I had managed to develop gave them a role in community, but not as themselves. What follows is the paper produced for that conference in which I began to move in a new direction and to see possibilities that Cohen's paper also pointed towards. The handicapped person, like Christ, is made in the image of God.

What are we to make of the mentally handicapped?

The handicapped challenge our assumptions about human nature. These assumptions are often connected with Christian doctrines about 'Man', which are often 'elitist' and the handicapped do not seem to make sense. Making sense of it is just as important as — indeed contributes to — coping with it, yet it is perhaps only in a theological context that the issues are likely to be faced.

The key paper given by Rex Ambler provides the proper starting-point. Even the handicapped are persons in the context of community. If the classical world threw up the definition 'man is a rational animal', it also produced a complementary thought: 'Man is a laughing animal'. The very first thing a baby does is to smile, then gurgle and laugh, and it is through these inarticulate and yet profound means of communication that we establish a relationship with a baby or a toddler. The same is true of the handicapped. Even with the severely limited, smiles, touch, laughter, etc. mean 'belonging'.

For this 'belonging' there is need for acceptance, but also for a sense of contributing. There is a real danger of care becoming patronage. There is all the difference in the world between being an 'object' of charity, and being allowed to help others. In personal relations, respect and reciprocity are as important as acceptance — we may take the black consciousness movement as a useful analogy. If we are not careful we force the handicapped to join society on our terms. If they are to be persons, we must learn to 'receive' from them. Brian Easter has always stressed the importance of 'friendship' for mentally handicapped people. We may also note the article by Jürgen Moltmann, 'The Liberation and Acceptance of the Handicapped' in *The Power of the Powerless* (SCM, 1983). The handicapped who understand and are capable like to do their bit, engaging for example in sponsored activities for people in need, just like others.

Theologically this is important: If we think of the idea of the body of Christ with its diversity of membership, each of which contributes to the whole; or reflect on the notion of 'original sin' which stresses our corporateness, our involvement in the *massa perditionis*, the fact that we are all in it together; or remember the importance of what we term 'corporate personality' in Old Testament; by considering all these examples, we can see that embedded in the Christian tradition is the idea that social realities mean collective responsibility for good and ill. The rediscovery of our corporateness seems to me to be essential for understanding 'atonement'. So the stress on the fact that we are persons in community is consonant both with Christian theology, and with the insights which come from relating to the handicapped.

It is important that we think through the consequences of this in terms of 'policy': where is the community appropriate to the handicapped? Is community care a way of enhancing their belonging to community or cramping it? What are the implications of taking friendship seriously — we all choose friends who share our interests, problems, etc.? Are we denying something about the handicapped when we seek 'normalisation' and try to integrate them into 'normal' society?

And these questions lead me to the shift of emphasis that I now want to introduce. In our enthusiasm for community, we must not lose sight of the individual, however much we

187

feel our culture has over-emphasised it. Individual responses are different, and individual needs are different. In the case of the handicapped this individuality is often even more marked than among so-called 'normal' people — no two have exactly the same combination of handicaps, and personality features are often manifest in an unusually exaggerated form. Lack of conformity to society's norms of behaviour is often the most difficult aspect of mental handicap. We must never ignore the fact that individuality is an important part of being a person, and indeed that privacy is a person's right. Despite the fact that any one of us may have different personalities in the context of different company and different relationships, and may sometimes wonder whether we are recognisably the same person in different communities, we acknowledge that in some mysterious way there is a continuity of identity as a person, independent of the various communities of which we are a part at different moments of our lives. And whether we like it or not, our culture does emphasise individuality — individual fulfilment, individual rights, self-determination, etc. While there may be an understandable desire to rediscover and to re-establish community, the status of the individual over against society's collectivities is still a very important issue, and affirmation of each 'person' has been an important emphasis in the Christian Gospel.

So I have come to see that there is a very important difference between affirming my son Arthur because of the place he has in the family community, what he has evoked in us, how he has contributed to our moral and spiritual progress and perceptions, and seeing that he is a child of God in his own right. The traditional 'doctrine of Man', as well as the natural assumptions about 'person' in our culture, involves a strong individualism.

So my purpose is to examine more traditional formulations and definitions within the Christian tradition, and see how the handicapped may or may not fit.

1. Christianity has tended to define humanity in terms of a 'perfect ideal'. In classic Christian doctrine, it is assumed that Adam was perfect. He fell from that perfection, but nevertheless the 'Doctrine of Man' traditionally begins with that ideal, trying to spell out what human perfection might be, and often in effect spelling out a very elitist ideal.

Parallel assumptions operate when it comes to understanding handicap. The very word, like the word '*disability*', suggests a *fall* away from what is perfect, whether we mean physical, mental, moral, psychological, or spiritual handicap. We operate as if we know what a perfect human being is, and the problems we are concerned with are to do with 'missing the mark'. Such assumptions are pervasive in a society which is geared to curing all ills, and prolonging youth — in fact, prolonging life at its most ideal — indefinitely. We belong to a culture which manifests refusal to accept the naturalness of old age, failing powers, death. Inevitably there is also refusal to accept the 'naturalness' of Down's Syndrome. It is taken to be an 'illness' or a 'mistake'. To abandon an 'ideological' approach to understanding humanity, and regain a sense of the naturalness of human mortality, vulnerability and frailty could do much to help with the acceptance of the handicapped as natural, and the development of a sense of identity with them.

But we have to face the facts that (1) some of the handicapped know they are not 'normal' and feel 'deprived'; and (2) the natural reaction among the non-handicapped is to seek cure, alleviation, etc. This is evident not just in the widespread search for 'magic methods' (Doman-Delacato, conductive education, etc.) but also in the instinctive desire for 'miracle' in Christian tradition.

189

It is easy to see how this ideology can be damaging. People's hopes are almost inevitably disappointed. There is a lack of reality in people's response to the situation. Yet can we relinquish some sense of the 'ideal'? The answer is probably not. It at least provides aims, and fuels the endeavour to do something. But we could perhaps do better at acknowledging its elusiveness and its indefinable quality. We could also do more to recognise and express our sense of common identity. After all we are all in the same case — we are all 'fallen' — none is perfect, no not one. . . . The doctrine of 'original sin' is in some ways a most compassionate doctrine.

2. There is also a tradition in Christianity which has defined humanity in terms of human potential, rather than original but lost ideal. John Hick, in *Evil and the God of love* (Macmillan 1966), called it the 'Irenaean' concept of the Fall after the early Christian bishop, Irenaeus, who first exploited the idea. Adam was not perfect but 'innocent'. He had the potential for maturity. Making mistakes is part of the maturing process.

This type of approach is also important: it can help us to grasp that the handicapped are 'different' not 'sub-'. Every single one has a potential of some kind. Quite apart from the theological dimensions of this approach, the sense that there is always potential has in fact been very important in the development of education for the handicapped, etc.

One result which might be seen as problematic, is that 'normalisation' tends to become the ideal. That is what people think they mean by developing potential. But does it really enhance a handicapped person's dignity as a human being to drill certain socially acceptable skills into that person? Could not the techniques of behaviour modification be as morally offensive as 'brain-washing' — depriv-

ing handicapped persons of their individuality and freedom? On the other hand, do the handicapped have the
'right' to self-determination and freedom, when they may
be a danger to themselves? What about the right to protection? Is 'normalisation' appropriate? This whole approach
raises many serious questions about the appropriateness of
community care, how to deal with the fact that handicapped people have sexual experience, whether access to
pornography, or violent videos, is to be denied, etc. In
practice, what does it mean to develop 'potential'?

There are also other less practical but more fundamental
questions to be asked about 'potential' and values. The
handicapped may have the positive potential to develop
gifts which are denied to the more sophisticated. By com-
parison, self-help skills may be a distraction from the development of other qualities. I recognise that what I am about
to suggest runs the risk of appearing sentimental — but the
basic trustfulness, lack of inhibitions, and that indefinable
virtue — simplicity — often seen in the mentally handicapped, may be the very qualities that it would be criminal
to educate out of them. This could be their potential — and
an area where the rest of us fail desperately. Within the
Christian tradition, there is an important critique of worldly
success values, and maybe the potential of the handicapped
which should be recognised and fostered is not to be like
the rest of us in our distrust and fear, but to be 'fools for
Christ'. It is instructive to observe the importance placed on
the handicapped in mediaeval society: the 'lunatics' who
take no thought for the morrow, and are no respecters of
persons, are 'God's apostles', the only incorruptible
members of society. For this they are to be valued and given
hospitality.

3. The Christian tradition has also defined what is essen-

tially human in terms of being made in the 'image of God', or being a 'child of God'.

Clearly it is possible to give elitist definitions of this — especially within the protestant tradition which demands personal commitment. Most serious is the demand for believer's baptism, which would on the face of it, exclude the handicapped (though see the remarkable study, *Let love be genuine.* . . Mental Handicap and the Church, edited by Faith Bowers, published by the Baptist Union, 1985). It is also possible to give sentimental definitions — as in the case of the Catholic tendency to see the 'soul peeping out through their eyes'. This both traps the handicapped in dependency, and puts off their being their true selves until they receive their reward in heaven. . . .

Yet in spite of these damaging tendencies, the idea has the potential to embrace positive insights under each of the heads previously discussed: every human being is in the same case, simply by being a child of God with enormous potential, in which unfortunately the image of God has been distorted, and so human community has been fragmented. The image of God is restored in the Body of Christ, in which every individual is affirmed for the bit they have to contribute to the total image, but none can claim to be the image of God on their own. Infants and the handicapped are properly baptised into this community. Here diversity among the members is as important as their unity; individuality is as important as community.

The realisation of God's image in human life and society is fragmentary because this world is 'penultimate' — morality, handicap, failure, wrongdoing, is part of life as we know it. Handicapped and non-handicapped alike, have the same basic needs, and the potential for further development together.

It is not generally known what a useful picture of human-

192

ity is to be found in the theology of the early Christian Fathers. They believed that humanity had a dual being — an animal nature, which made human beings part of the natural creation, formed from the dust, as the Bible suggested (It is a great pity that this was forgotten in 19th century reaction to Darwin's suggestion that we are descended from monkeys!); and also a spiritual nature, the image of God, being endowed with God's Spirit. Traditionally, this latter element was identified with human spirituality understood in highly rationalistic terms. But perhaps the idea is adaptable and 'rings true' with our own perception of the mystery of human being. We are descended from the apes, but we are 'laughing animals' — we only thrive in community. We are the 'image of God', but that means we are reflections of God in different ways, and the whole image is never quite put together (except in Christ). The handicapped, even those so extremely handicapped and lacking in responsiveness as to manifest a kind of death in the midst of life, reflect aspects of God which the rest of us do not, and we need the discernment to respond to, respect and honour their unique witness. After all, they are vulnerable as Christ was vulnerable. They are where most would rather not be.

In 1988 I was invited to give the Christian Education Movement lecture in Birmingham. It was interesting how the material in the last chapter and in this wove together under the title: 'Made in the image of God: the challenge of the handicapped to the Christian understanding of human nature.'

The lecture began by outlining the difficulties of integrating the mentally handicapped into society, using many incidents or examples found earlier in this book. The relatively easier task of accepting the physically handicapped was acknowledged: we can see or imagine a 'real person' beyond the physical handicap. Traditional Christian doctrines collude with this. After drawing on Mary Douglas again, this collusion was explored: the 'perfect ideal' encourages the characterisation of handicap as 'unnatural', the emphasis on 'potential' encourages 'normalisation', so failing to acknowledge 'difference', the idea of the 'image of God' has usually been understood in terms of the 'mind' or 'soul', and so encourages elitism and exclusion. So the climax was tackling the question: what is the creative way of handling the anomaly?

It was suggested that the answers already exist within the Christian tradition but need to be made explicit. In the first place, accepting the fact of difference within the human community should not pose a problem: in Christ there is neither Jew nor Greek, slave nor free, male nor female, and we should add, black nor white, able-bodied and handicapped. The suggestion that the image of God is not complete in any individual but only in corporate humanity with all its adversity was taken up again. Within Christianity, Christ alone is the true image of God, but in him we are a new creation, and we are the Body of Christ. So exclusion, re-definition and denial of the handicapped are all excluded: they belong as themselves, with all their difference.

And this means, secondly, that the handicapped contribute to the 'image of God'. Already in the Christian tradition, the image of God is seen in Christ who was marginalised, vulnerable, exposed to the sins of the human race, and suffered on behalf of all. Unwittingly the handicapped are often found in the same position, the scapegoats of a society that cannot acknowledge their value. This association is far from sentimental, for the cross was a messy business. So was the holocaust and the centuries-old suffering of the Jews. So is handicap. Christ stands for the victims, for the presence of God being with the victims so that the whole can be redeemed. And in a sense the handicapped stand for Christ in our midst.

Thirdly, 'sacralising the anomaly' is the way of redemption, and we have to allow the handicapped to effect our 'conversion'. Only being honest about our ambiguous feelings, and then allowing ourselves to be changed by entering into a reciprocal relationship with the handicapped, can be effective. That change will involve a 'transvaluation', the recognition that our success values have to be put into a different perspective by other values. John Chrysostom used to preach that the rich depend on the poor for their salvation. In a sense we normal people are the rich: our judgment comes in the way we respond to the challenge of the handicapped, they provide us with an opportunity for repentance, and so we depend on them for our redemption.

Note
    The papers given at the 1986 Spring Conference were duplicated but are now out of print. The CEM lecture is unpublished.

Chapter 10

THE DARK SIDE OF HOPE

The dark side of hope is disappointment.

People in contact with the handicapped have to learn to accept disappointment, but they are given little help to do so. My first essay in this area was a paper for an earlier Pastoral Studies Conference, and the second an essay for a volume on Special Education. These are reproduced below in reverse order but in their original form, despite the fact that this means a certain amount of repetition and retelling of the story. But these essays seem worth including because they affirm more sharply than anything else that there is no room for sentiment, at least not so far as this life is concerned.

The final section draws on an unpublished paper to offer some reflections on the nature of Christian hope, setting the issue in the wider context of hope for the world. The dark side of hope becomes the birth-pangs of the new creation. . . .

The Education of Arthur

With a very severely handicapped child, the fundamental problem is the gradual coming to terms with how limited the child is. One always hopes and imagines that things will be better than they are. The thrust of all services for the mentally handicapped and their families is towards positive progress and success. This is no doubt an excellent reaction against past practice. But for the family with a child as profoundly handicapped as Arthur, it can in fact create more pressures, both practical and emotional, than it is possible to cope with. It increases the sense of 'failure', and

196

creates unnecessary 'guilt' and feelings of inadequacy. I guess the same can be true of teachers too.

Arthur was a full-term baby but born at premature weight. We innocent first-time parents had no suspicions that things were wrong, though experienced medical people clearly knew from the start that development in the womb had been retarded. At eight months he was diagnosed as microcephalic. His 'education' began some six months later when after moving to a different part of the country, our new GP put us in contact with the Inspector for Special Education, and he introduced us to the Dolman-Delacato method. Our lives became dominated by the need to stimulate Arthur, and do 'patterning' with him twice a day. At that stage we were desperate to do anything to increase his potential. But then he was an only child, and we still had hope.

At a remarkably early age (given what we now know about his disabilities) Arthur learned to crawl. We had been led to believe that mobility would make all the difference to his learning capacity. He enjoyed movement, and at times would hare around on all fours. But it was only for the sensation. He remained profoundly unresponsive, and if we are honest, there was little eye contact. We kidded ourselves he responded more than he actually did. He was extremely limited in terms of play, using only various rattles. With these he developed a very complex set of hand movements, but never really succeeded with anything else, in spite of efforts to prompt and interest. He was incapable of sitting up in balance, and despite the crawling ability, he did not acquire the capacity to see a favourite toy at the other side of the room and go to fetch it. He had no instinct to put anything in his mouth, and feeding remained a persistent problem.

So the ability to crawl advanced his capacity in one area

only, and masked the profundity of his disability. It fed hope, ultimately to make the disillusion, and the physical problems, more trying. It would take years for these 'side-effects' to become apparent. In his teens we experienced weeks of discomfort with his legs in plaster stretching contracted tendons, and for a while afterwards a complete loss of independent mobility. Further physical consequences of his tendency to settle on the floor in a particular position and stay there for hours are still creating problems. We are in a 'Catch-22' situation, and in fact always were. But I lived for years blaming myself for letting him 'sit' on his legs in a kneeling position, though that was an almost inevitable consequence of having encouraged him to crawl early. He did at last crawl around looking for his favourite toy; but his dawning initiative came too late. Physically he has not developed the muscles for him to be able to take advantage of his 'progress' — in fact, his body is now so twisted that his 'walking' (with assistance) is regressing.

Meanwhile number two arrived, and as parents we began to realise that our lives could not be dominated by the supposed needs of the handicapped child. It took a long time to find a balanced perspective, but the next one was abnormally bright, and as soon as he could crawl was into everything, including Arthur's exercises! Refusal of attention would clearly create deep jealousy. The compromises had to begin. I am convinced now that such compromises actually reflect maturity in the parents of handicapped children: the desire to 'do something' easily becomes obsessive and deeply unhealthy. Programmes like Dolman-Delacato exploit the natural reactions of desperate parents, and can create psychological blockages to the achievement of balance in attitude and in family life.

Pre-school experience included time for Arthur in a Day Nursery, again to widen his stimulation by being with normal children. But once more looking back I am sceptical about how much he really gained. I suspect he became more nervous of people, because toddlers barge in and he was defenceless. I suspect we also made mistakes about the relationship with his younger brother, and it would have been better if both had been in the same Nursery group — but like everything else that is water under the bridge and one is wiser by hindsight, unfortunately. My guess is that out of the home, the younger one would have protected Arthur rather than being jealous of him, and we lost a positive opportunity.

Arthur was admitted to Special School at the age of five (remarkable in those days!). He remained in the same class for years, and the same school until he left at eighteen. Effectively teachers were struggling with the same self-help skills when he finished as when he started — notably feeding and toiletting. The reality is that at twenty-one he is still in nappies and still has to be fed, and you could say that no progress was made at all over all those years. In fact in various little ways, Arthur has developed a lot. Even since leaving school he has become noticeably more responsive and curious about things going on around him. He gets bored by long periods at home, and enjoys going out. That never used to be the case — he was happiest just left alone in peace, and insecure in an unfamiliar environment. This gradually developing responsiveness has no doubt been helped by our insistence on his going out and away from home and adapting to different environments, despite his sometimes adverse reactions, but apart from this, it is not easy to say that he has benefitted by any of his education, certainly not in terms of passing any notable milestones.

That may sound hard, and it may sound as though as parents we are dissatisfied with what he received. That is by no means the case. We always felt that the school did its very best for our son, and was remarkably adaptive in coping with his most difficult stages, when we were all under pressure. It is not a criticism but a statement of reality, and I feel that that reality needs to be faced. What teachers need, as well as parents, is help with coping with 'failure'. Our ideology is so 'success-oriented', and 'success' defined in terms of constant little bits of 'progress' towards 'normality', that the reality of non-progress is far too demoralising to admit. But sometimes it cannot be avoided. I remember the School Doctor telling me one day how she had had to help the staff to face the fact that when Arthur had a fit and did not breathe, nothing could be done, and he might just die. . . . I was glad of that realism, and I would have liked to see more of it.

That is easily said, not so easily put into practice. Parents and teachers will all be at different 'emotional' stages in their developing capacity to cope with handicap. If help with coming to terms with the reality of failure is offered at the wrong moment, it can cause profound hurt. When a Specialist told me I must not let the normal child suffer for the sake of the handicapped one, I couldn't take it at the time; but it wasn't long before I recognised its wisdom. I think what I most want to say is that there are times when pressure for progress, pressure for collaboration between school and home towards particular goals, can be more than the family can take, and it is vital that those involved in the education of the profoundly handicapped be sensitive to what is and is not possible.

Our roughest period was during the babyhood of our third. His arrival meant that yet again we were coping with two babies, and one of them increasingly large, and at that stage extremely difficult. Arthur went through a profoundly distressing period, in which he would resist all handling — dressing, bathing, changing nappies, eating, even loving!

In many ways he went backwards rather than forwards. He could not communicate what was wrong, and I responded with all the desperate emotions of a young mother with an interminably crying baby. No-one could help. Doctors prescribed sedatives — to no effect. By now we had lost all hope. Survival was all we asked for.

Yet some professionals were still talking about progress and development, and what we should be doing to encourage him to feed himself. . . . It was utterly inappropriate, and I for one couldn't take it and was left feeling guilty and inadequate. Hindsight has again helped: Arthur over-reacts to all discomfort and we now believe he was cutting his second teeth. We have been through patches of similar behaviour recently, and we reckon it is wisdom teeth! It is still hard to take, but now we believe there is a different Arthur who will re-emerge in a while. Then we could see no point in his miserable existence, and it went on for years. Progress was non-existent during that period.

Emerging from all that, I am convinced that there are far more valuable things than 'progress', and pressure for 'progress' can actually get in the way of developing those more valuable things. What matters far more is trust and respect, a relationship in which love can flourish because it is relaxed and accepting. Love for a handicapped child can be possessive and dictatorial to the point of damage if our aims and hopes are inappropriate. In the present climate, that is much more likely than leaving them be without any stimulation.

Of course it is hard to know whether things could have been different. But I do think that Arthur's progress has to a large extent been 'inbuilt', and a lot of our efforts to force it have in fact created more problems for him and us. He learned to resist our efforts, and to be utterly uncooperative. He became distrustful of people. I guess my own anxiety as a mother made his distressed reactions more marked. Things are far better since I have been able to relax, accept the reality of his extreme handicap, stop blaming myself for making things worse by my own mistakes, enjoy him for what he is, and respect him enough to leave him alone when he doesn't want my attention.

A theological critique of therapeutic optimism
>   All flesh is grass
>   and all its glory like the flower of grass.
>   The grass withers and the flower falls. . . .

The Bible is thoroughly realistic and natural about death — apart from those passages promising resurrection, which are late and always treat it as a creative miracle, so confirming the naturalness of death.

In a sense our post-Christian society is equally naturalistic, and yet within certain circles, especially those concerned with pastoral studies, there has developed serious discussion about the *un*naturalness of modern attitudes to death, and the widespread social conspiracy to deny its reality.

I do not wish to pursue that particular discussion further except to say that it provides an instructive backcloth to the subject with which I am concerned, and in my view shares some of the same roots. We would all be agreed, I think, that the widespread loss of religious meaning is one contributory cause, but another is an unrealistic and over-confident humanism that insists upon human autonomy and encourages the cultivation of success values in all areas of life. In this context, death cannot be admitted because it would be an admission of failure. The effect of this upon medically-related professions is another topic that has been previously explored.

What I wish to suggest is that the success values of our society have also caused a lack of realism in relation to other situations, and that a deeper appreciation of the realistic biblical perspective would help to redress the balance. Because science has apparently been so successful — particularly medical science so successful in ridding us of so many of the common ills of human life, so that infant mortality has dropped drastically and length of life expanded beyond belief compared with even a century ago — the delusion of our society is that humanity can resolve all its problems, and *something* can be done about *everything*. Even if we cannot yet cure a given condition, research presses on in the confidence that one day we will, and meanwhile effective therapies are devised to ameliorate its effects. At the very least this keeps up morale. So programmes are clothed in ambitious quasi-scientific language, what is done is given a moral sanction by appeal to the enhancement of human dignity, and an effective diversion from facing up to the reality of the situation is created. These attitudes are neatly encapsulated in the phrase Stephen Pattison gave me, 'therapeutic optimism'. I am not an expert in these matters. I am simply the parent of a severely handicapped son who has experienced the attitudes of doctors, educators, social workers and fellow-parents, and who knows about Doman-Delacato, behaviour modification, Makaton and various other programmes through this personal connection. I will leave others to analyse and generalise the point I am making, which I am sure applies far more widely than in the field of Mental Handicap. What I want to do is to suggest that there is a whole set of unrealistic assumptions being made about the nature of human beings and about appropriate values. Luckily human beings usually behave better than they theorise, and many workers do instinctively what is appropriate in spite of it all. But would it not be better to get consciously acknowledged aims right? I suggest that there are biblical perspectives, traditional doctrines and popular Christian attitudes of the past which bear upon this, and that theological reflection can contribute a more realistic perspective on humanity and human achievement.

There is an Irish tramp who calls on us fairly regularly, and his parting words are often, 'I always say a prayer for you, lady'. I find this fascinating and moving, because it reflects a view that goes right back to the time of the early church, namely that the rich are dependent upon the poor for their salvation. True this idea has all too often degenerated into simple encouragement of almsgiving which so easily becomes patronising charity, but in its original form it emphasised mutuality rather than individual moral achievement: the poor have a vital role in the economy of salvation. It is often thought that the affirmation of every individual is a characteristically Christian view, and there is some truth in this. The value of even the least in the sight of God is an important emphasis. But moral achievement, like any other achievement, academic, aesthetic, athletic or what have you, is a worldly value and more Stoic than Christian. The value of mutual responsibility for one another is deeply written into the legislation for society in the Old Testament, and worked out more profoundly in the New Testament understanding of Church community, especially the Pauline idea of the Body of Christ. Quite apart from the well-known texts stressing the diverse contributions of each member, and the hymn to love in I Cor. 13, there are the passages in which Paul pleads for the strong to respect the weak.

This is not the place for detailed exposition, and in any case it has all been said before. In the field of social responsibility, such values have entered the discussion, and some at least worry that non-achievers are marginalised in our society. But suppose we consider appropriate aims in relation to the handicapped. Society admires the handicapped achiever — the blind student at University, the wheelchair-bound marathon-runner. This kind of thing therefore provides the model. Most people who deal with handicapped persons look for the small triumphs, and achieving maximum possible potential is regarded as the aim by good parents and good professionals. Progress and self-help is assumed to enhance dignity as well as increase social acceptability.

But does self-help, if it has been mechanically drilled into behaviour and is merely the response of an automaton, actually increase dignity? Isn't a relaxed and caring relationship, an ability to let persons be themselves, and an admission of mutual dependence, a greater value? Isn't behaviour modification, however successful in increasing social acceptability, a way of manipulation and a denial of true humanity? Can we allow achievement to be the be-all-and-end-all? What kind of triumph is appropriate? Society measures triumph in terms of preserving life at all costs, developing full potential, overcoming the odds. But might not the real triumph be the ability to receive from one another, to discover interdependence, to find values which make success and death equally irrelevant? Should we not allow the handicapped to stimulate questioning about the value of autonomy, and look for other forms of transformation? Whether it happens that way — that is, by the handicapped helping us to re-discover forgotten perspectives — or the other way, namely by the Christian tradition helping us to criticise current attitudes, does not really matter. It is the coming together of the two that is important. The individual has value and dignity not as a result of personal achievement, but in relation to the community.

To take up another point, a good many years ago Metropolitan Anthony Bloom staggered a student audience on this campus with his suggestion that it was appropriate to live life as if tomorrow you would die. His is not the only voice proclaiming such wisdom, but such voices are relatively rare and difficult to hear, a far cry from the persistence of this theme in the popular philosophies of the ancient world and the wisdom of the Bible. I suppose when life was as precarious for most people as it is now in the Third World, and when even for the privileged, expectation of life was about half what it is now, it was easier to live with a continuous sense of human mortality and dependence. Certainly confidence in life going on and human ability to conquer all has never been so widespread — in spite of the experience of two World Wars and the shadow of the Bomb.

For biblical wisdom, human beings are dust and to dust they will return. It is only the power of God which keeps one in being. Humanity is entirely dependent on his will to keep one alive. Human success depends on the 'fear of the Lord', whether it be the power of kings or the wisdom of the wise or the prosperity of farmer or businessman. There is no immortality. Life is a miracle, and resurrection a miraculous renewal of life by God. All life is a privilege not a right. There is no expectation that as things are, human beings can create utopia or solve all problems or reach perfection. For the wolf to dwell with the lamb and the leopard to lie down with the kid, for the lion to eat straw like the ox and the toddler to put his hand in an adder's den, there has to be a miraculous re-creation.

I think it is time we heard some of this again. Of course the Bible also speaks of human responsibility given by God. But is it not vital that we come to terms with human limitations, with human inability to put everything right? In

206

the field of handicap, it is usually recognised that no cure is possible, and that learning to accept the situation is the only realism. But then morale is kept up by the kind of therapeutic activism I have already described. Of course great advances have been made, as in so many other areas of human life, and it is right we should acknowledge them. It *is* better to do something than fatalistically to leave the handicapped child in bed inevitably to become a cabbage. But do we not need to come clean about the limits of human competence? If we do not, then despair and disillusion is inevitable.

Maybe we only dare face up to it if we are granted a faith in the reality and goodness of God that puts our own frailty and mortality in deeper perspective. But if we were to face up to it, it might help us to recognise the handicapped (not to mention other vulnerable and marginalised persons) as a true embodiment of the human condition, a revelation and a comment upon the rest of us, if only we can discern it and make the right kind of identification. This insight could enhance the acceptance of such persons and the fostering of that mutuality of which I have spoken. We are none of us perfect. We share the same basic needs — food, drink, sleep, love. We have the same instinctive desire for life, the same ultimate end in death, the same frailty, the same vulnerability. Even the most successful are not demigods — in fact, we miss true humanity by looking for it where there is a danger of divine pretensions.

Which conveniently brings me to my final point: humanity is flawed not perfect. Someone commented after a recent sermon of mine that they had not thought before about the corruptibility of goodness. Anyone who has attempted to study the letters of Paul, however, will have had to face up to precisely this point. In the sermon I had used an example from *Bleak House*, namely the character of

Mrs Pardiggle whom Dickens describes as 'much distin-
guished for rapacious benevolence'. Caricature or not, it
rings horribly true of the world's 'do-gooders'.

The theme of tragic drama from the ancient world to
Shakespeare and beyond, has been 'pride comes before a
fall' or *hybris* brings its own *nemesis*. All human greatness is
flawed, even moral goodness. A human being who challenges the gods is in for it. The Bible contains the same
theme, in its well-known universal myths, Adam and the
Tower of Babel, and in its prophecy, notably Isaiah's taunt
of the king of Babylon:

> How are you fallen from heaven, O day star, son of the dawn!
> How you are cut down to the ground, you who laid the
> nations low. You said in your heart, 'I will ascend to heaven;
> above the stars of God I will set my throne on high. . . . I will
> ascend above the heights of the clouds. I will make myself
> like the Most High!' But you are brought down to Sheol, to
> the depth of the Pit.

That sin is not just wickedness but the corruption of goodness is particularly clear in the Gospel's attack on hypocrisy,
and Paul's critique of salvation by works. God may have
given human beings responsibility, but in practice that
privilege has never been used wisely or well, and it has
become a cliché that power corrupts. Success and achievement is distinctly ambiguous. All this provides a radical
critique of our modern claims to autonomy (*pace* Kant and
Don Cupitt).

In spite of its conformity to the world, Christianity has
historically thrown up strange contrary movements critical
of worldly success values. The monastic movement is the
obvious example, but not so well-known perhaps is the odd
development of this whereby some ascetics became 'fools
for Christ', deliberately concealing themselves in the guise

of witless and irresponsible beggars, living on trust. Knowing this I was fascinated when my attention was drawn to the comments of the mediaeval poet William Langland on those we would call mentally ill or handicapped: for him the 'lunatics' who take no thought for the morrow, and do not kow-tow to anyone, are 'God's apostles', the only incorruptible members of society. On these grounds they are to be valued and given hospitality. They perform a very special service to society by being a comment upon the attitudes of everyone else.

May I suggest that our society needs to rediscover the value of fools and the contribution of non-achievers to an alternative set of human values. The way forward is to modify 'therapeutic optimism', not losing its positive contributions, but tempering it with a realistic awareness of human frailty, corruptibility, mortality, mutual dependence and dependence on God. The interplay of biblical and traditional Christian perspectives with the practical realities of dealing with the handicapped and the vulnerable cannot but call in question our humanist assumptions and values.

Towards a realistic hope

The dark side of hope is disappointment. Is there then no hope? What is appropriate Christian hope? Perhaps we can begin to find an answer by exploring the so-called 'eschatology' of the New Testament, its picture of the 'Last Things'. One of the most intriguing things is the sense of 'now' and 'not yet' found throughout its pages. The present reality is of a world subject to corruption and decay, but the future 'Kingdom of God' is anticipated in Jesus, and the new creation has begun in Christ.

Suppose we take Paul as our primary example: 'Kingdom of God' is not one of Paul's favourite phrases, yet he uses it in common with other early Christian writers, and in his letters it occurs in such a way as to link the promise of the future reign of God with present experience of the Spirit, with present lifestyles and priorities. The kingdom appears to be present in embryo in the elect who have the gift of the Spirit, who constitute the new covenant community and are the Body of Christ. Whether Pauline or not, Colossians 1.13 sums up Paul's view: 'He has delivered us from the dominion of darkness and transferred us to the kingdom of his beloved Son.'

It cannot therefore be said that Paul's view of the kingdom is simply a projection onto the heavens: it is not simply otherworldly or spiritual, and it does not imply a simple rejection of material existence, despite the suggestion that flesh and blood cannot inherit it. It is eschatological in the sense that it is effected by God when the old order is brought to an end and the new order created. It is certainly not to be 'achieved' by human effort. But there is a continuity between the body of flesh and blood and the spiritual body like the continuity between seed and plant, and there is a continuity between the old world and the new, the new being anticipated in the midst of the old. The kingdom means the redemption and transformation of the kind of existence known already. It has an ethical dimension in that it is anticipated in the Christian way of life, in obedience to the will of God through the Spirit which has created new hearts and minds in believers, so producing love, joy, peace and righteousness.

In fact Paul's use of the phrase 'kingdom of God' appears to cohere with that frequently observed feature of his understanding, the 'over-lapping of the ages'. It seems that Paul in common with many others at the time, expected the fulfilment of the prophecies to mean God's final intervention to wind up the present evil age and bring in the new, and what he believed to have happened with the coming of Christ was the initiation of that process. God's wrath and righteousness were alike being revealed: the cross marked the beginning of the final woes, and the Spirit the beginning of the new creation. Yet the present evil age was not yet over, and the final consummation still belonged to the future.

So there is this tension in Paul's language between the 'now' and the 'not yet': on the one hand, believers are already justified, sanctified, adopted as sons of God and heirs of the kingdom; on the other hand they have to become what they already are, and there is plenty of advice about what that means in terms of personal purity, relationships in the church community, etc. They cannot live in sin so that grace may abound. The tenses in Romans 6 are instructive: having died with Christ they will rise with him. Christian believers will be saved, they are awaiting their redemption; yet that future has to be lived in the present.

An exactly parallel tension between the 'now' and the 'not yet' is particularly associated with the kingdom in the Synoptic Gospels, and with 'eternal life' in the Johannine literature. The problems of relating future eschatology and realised eschatology constitute a long-standing area of discussion in New Testament scholarship, and need not be considered in detail here. Suffice it to say that the imminence of the kingdom appears to be the burden of Jesus' message in the Synoptic Gospels, and sometimes it appears to be present in his activity, especially his confrontation with the powers of evil. His proclamation is the fulfilment of the prophecies and of all the hopes of Israel for God's reign on earth; yet his life is not 'Messianic' in the accepted sense, and there is a constant note of looking forward to the consummation of God's kingdom, the same old tension between the 'now' and the 'not yet'. Similarly in John's

Gospel, 'eternal life' is sometimes spoken of as a present possession, sometimes as a future reward; it appears to mean the 'life of the age to come' rather than simply life that goes on for ever, in other words it is the kind of life to be lived in God's kingdom, which is in a sense already available. The phrase 'eternal life', like 'kingdom of God', does not seem particularly characteristic of Paul, and yet is found as a kind of 'formula' in a number of places, and its usage parallels that of the 'kingdom language'.

So where the Gospels seem to identify the coming of the kingdom, which is nevertheless still to come, with the appearance of the Christ, Paul seems to focus the anticipation of the kingdom in the gift of the Spirit and the life of the church. The kingdom is present in embryo in the 'body of Christ' which is the new covenant community. Yet Paul has no illusions about the realities of life in those communities: his letters are an appeal to work out their salvation with fear and trembling, to become what they are.

If this is the New Testament view of the way things are, the idealistic claims so often found among Christian activists, whether for development, for peace or for political liberation, seem somewhat out of line. Despite the declining influence of the churches, there is an unrealistic and uncharacteristic spirit of 'optimism' around — even in the charismatic movement, especially those groups promising health, wealth and success if you only let God into your life — an optimism that speaks of the present reality of the kingdom as if all the problems of the world could be wafted away if we only found the right 'formula'. Whether it be 'the power of prayer' or 'the revolution' or the scrapping of nuclear weapons. This attitude is at variance both with one's reading of history and one's reading of the scriptures. One cannot help wondering whether it may not be basically a 'sell-out' to the spirit of the age — the optimistic utopianism created by the real, though temporal, successes of science, medicine and technology.

But speaking of the spirit of the age, alongside this tendency to an unrealistic optimism about the future, we also commonly observe a profound pessimism, a sense that things are not what they used to be — memories are short, and the social conditions of Victorian England, or the time of war and depression are forgotten; the scenes on the television screens make bad news all too present and contemporary. There is a massive discontent and despair about society, about violence, about economic forces — there seems something inevitable about the passing on of social inadequacy or communal conflict from one generation to another. Such pessimism is also misplaced and unrealistic: surely nothing quite compares to the institutionalised violence of discipline in the English Navy when able-bodied men were liable to be pressed into service, and suffered little better conditions than those carted off in the slave trade. There are ways in which things have improved and our moral sensibilities have developed: genocide may still go on, but at least it is no longer something to boast about.

In this kind of way, perspectives may be shifted by taking a longer view of things, but also by respecting the tension and balance within the Christian tradition, the tension between the 'now' and the 'not yet' observed in the very earliest Christian writings. Christianity has in fact had a variety of hopes concerning the future, the relation of this world and heaven or the world to come, the timing of the End. Most involve abandoning one or other of the poles of this tension.

In struggling to come to terms both with the proclamation of the kingdom as a present reality and with the tragic experience of human vulnerability and mortality, I have found this tension instructive and helpful. Naturally the espousal of the eschatological views of the New Testament in all their strangeness is difficult, but whatever one makes of it theoretically or philosophically, the position outlined 'rings true' to experience and the realities of our existence.

For whether we like it or not, there are things we cannot change; there are handicaps we cannot overcome, and old age eventually gets us all; and what is the point of delaying death when we shall in fact all die? We cannot now un-invent nuclear weapons, so there can be no long term security. There is no hope of an earthly utopia, and human attempts to create a perfect world nearly always go bad on us — one only has to think of the disturbing results of the grand programme of slum clearance: intentions good, outcome socially disastrous. Much of the problems of famine and underdevelopment are the inadvertent results of 'progress' and over-population. Over so many areas of life, the very effort to do good seems to end up going wrong, and this applies on a corporate scale, not only in the case of the proverbial Pharisee who in seeking moral uprightness commits the sin of pride and self-righteousness. Human life is subject to bondage and corruption, however unfashion-able it may be to suggest this.

And yet this is not the whole story: human life is shot through with a kind of magic, miracles of grace, genuine change, real hope at the penultimate level. Against all the odds, the slave trade was abolished. There are little antici-pations of the kingdom, if only we have the eyes to discern them, and we look in the right places. The over-optimism and over-pessimism characteristic of contemporary atti-tudes is to some extent born out of ever-increasing expec-tations, and those expectations need to be put into the right perspective.

So Paul gives us a perspective on things, a perspective in which we cannot escape both the 'now' and the 'not yet': for

(1) human nature and human society, even within the church, is corrupted but redeemable; (2) the present evil age is a reality but it is not the whole of reality; (3) God is trustworthy and is at work in the world, despite appearances; (4) human effort cannot produce the kingdom, but we may be called to be fellow-workers for the kingdom and to participate in effecting God's plan of redemption; (5) we can experience now what life in the kingdom of God is to be, and yet we cannot take it for granted — it is always under threat and always has to be struggled for; (6) individuals need to be changed, but that change is only evident in the resulting community of relationships — neither personal salvation alone, nor structural change alone, can bring kingdom values into effect; (7) neither optimism nor pessimism is appropriate — the Christian virtues are faith, hope and love: these transcend the present, and yet are anticipated within the present order; (8) the pattern of Christ's death and resurrection means that Christian hope is never a bland confidence — for Christian faith is in a God who can bring life out of death, and death has to be accepted for the transformation to take place. In other words, while there is a relationship between the values and hopes of the world and those of the kingdom, there is also a fundamental critique of a worldly utopia effected by worldly programmes of reform.

The dark side of hope is the pain and judgment involved in the world's labour to give birth to God's new creation. Both God's righteousness and his wrath are revealed in Christ. And the Christian hope is neither for final solutions now, nor pie in the sky when you die, but rather hope for ultimate new creation guaranteed by anticipations now.

Chapter 11

THE DARK SIDE OF DISCIPLESHIP

What does it mean to be true to one's vocation? What does it mean to identify with the poor and oppressed? *The Story in Part A* hinted at these questions but did not explore them. Telling one's story always means selecting what seems relevant to the occasion or the audience at the time. But the theological dynamic of the story demands attention to questions which do not seem at first sight directly relevant to Arthur — except in so far as that story might be read as a justification of my own spiritual journey, and Arthur becomes a mere instrument in it, a trial or wilderness experience contributing to my theological reflection and ministerial formation. Is it not offensive to suggest that a man was born blind so that Jesus could demonstrate miraculous powers (John 9.3ff)? Is it not offensive that Arthur was born handicapped for my spiritual benefit?

Of course he has been of fundamental importance, and perhaps we should begin by exploring that aspect. What has he to say through me? Some things have already come out along the way: the importance of perceiving where true values lie by contrast with success, the fact that those in relationship with the handicapped receive from them, the importance of identifying ourselves as handicapped people. . . . But I guess there is something more.

Identification with the poor and oppressed

The Cathedral was full, full of successful women gathered for their annual service: the United Kingdom Federation of Business and Professional Women. I mounted the pulpit steps. We had heard the lections for the Second

Sunday after Easter with their emphasis on 'feeding my sheep' and 'tending my flock'. How easy to encourage myself and all these successful women in paternalistic (or should I say maternalistic) attitudes! But my text was from I Peter 5.5: 'Clothe yourselves, all of you, with humility toward one another, for "God opposes the proud, but gives grace to the humble".'

We began with Mrs Pardiggle. *Bleak House* was serialised on Television at the time, but they had 'cut' Mrs Pardiggle, Dickens' brilliant take-off of the Victorian bossy do-gooder whose charitable ministrations made the recipients shiver in their shoes. We enjoyed the caricature together.

Then I suggested that it is very important for successful people like ourselves to be reminded of what it is like to be on the underside, how hard it can be, how demeaning, to be on the receiving end, and suggested that Dickens helps us to sense it. 'As it happens,' I continued, 'I can speak from both sides. I am a social worker's client, the recipient of social benefits, and a vulnerable patient — or at least the parent of one. I am also a professional woman, a teacher and a minister. I am convinced that the way I play my pastoral and leadership roles have been significantly affected by my experience of being on the receiving end, or if they have not, they should have been.'

I tried to share something of what it meant to be identified with the disadvantaged and receive from the people who are marginalised in our society, and suggested that humility toward one another meant respecting people 'under us', and expecting to receive from people 'under us': only in this way is it possible to lead without imposing constraint and without domineering over those for whom we have to care and those we have to direct.

Picking up from the lesson a verse or two later, I suggested that to do this we have to be watchful. Maybe we do

217

not any more imagine that the devil is prowling around like a roaring lion seeking someone to devour, but whether we put it that way or not, the Christian insight is that goodness is easily corruptible. That power corrupts has become a cliché, but the really insidious thing is the fact that goodness corrupts or is so easily corruptible. As long as we think we are self-sufficient, the danger is real. The ancient Stoics and modern humanists have one thing in common — a tremendous faith in the self-sufficiency and moral autonomy of the human individual. But any human being who has lost the capacity to receive from others is on the road to becoming Mrs Pardiggle. We should thank God for satirists and comedians, since if no-one else can take us down a peg or two, perhaps they can.

Sin is goodness corrupted, and that kind of sin is far more insidious than downright evil, I repeated. Those of us who mean well and have power over others need to be wary, and I went on to speak of the 'great Shepherd of the sheep' who humbled himself unto death and suffered for his flock, suggesting that God himself knows what it is like to be on the receiving end. 'I'd never thought of goodness as corruptible before,' said a departing member of the congregation. How desperately shallow is our self-knowledge!

I am grateful that with Arthur I have been on the receiving end. What does it mean to identify with the poor and the oppressed? There are those who feel called to abandon privilege in order to do this. I honour them, though sometimes their moral 'high-horse' is so threatening it alienates those it seeks to convince. Middle-class 'lefties' are all too prone to romanticise the 'working-class' in the way clerics have romanticised the poor down the ages. Some of us find ourselves constrained by circumstance to be among the élite, to bear the label 'oppressors', though we seem powerless to do anything about our social position. Whatever we do about the structures of society, however angry we may feel on behalf of the 'outcast', the most important thing is to share the 'soul' of the marginalised, and endeavour to keep up lines of communication between the inner city and the outer suburb, the low and the high, the poor and the rich, the spiritually rich and the spiritually poor. Patronising is the result of not being humble enough in spirit to receive from those who are in worldly terms 'below', but in other respects often 'above'.

For reconciliation involves belonging to one another, and if the Christian Gospel is about reconciliation the breaking down of barriers lies at the very heart of the ministerial vocation. This has been driven home for me both by sharing in the work of the Centre for Black and White Christian Partnership, and by sharing in the life of inner city churches, as recounted earlier. Arthur sometimes exemplifies the difficulties.

I was invited to preach on an occasion when trainees for ministry were exploring disability. We began from the text, 'There is neither Jew nor Greek, there is neither slave nor free, there is neither male nor female', and these days, I suggested, we would most of us naturally go on, 'black nor white, rich nor poor, Catholic nor Anglican, Orthodox nor Methodist, for you are all one in Christ Jesus.' But would we include the able and the disabled, I enquired. Then I challenged them with what had happened: when I had received the invitation, I had responded not only with a sense of privilege, but a sense of joy because it provided an occasion to bring Arthur along to join in the worship of the community without any feeling of intrusion. I had intended not to refer to his presence, but I had been made aware that some were wondering about my motives in bringing him — was he a kind of visual aid?

So what had seemed natural no longer had done — I had

219

had to examine myself. I had had to admit to myself that on any other occasion I would have made arrangements for his care. I had had to admit that maybe I did want them all to face reality after talking about it all day. So he was to be a kind of visual aid. So I would have to make other arrangements.

But the decision had left me with a dreadful sense of loss, and a genuine discovery — that what his presence really meant was a celebration of our wholeness together and that that celebration was essential to what I had to say. If I brought some Pentecostal friends to share in a celebration of unity, would that be a visual aid, I asked. If I brought some black friends to share in a celebration of our oneness in Christ, would that be a visual aid? Arthur belongs, I insisted — he is baptised and belongs to Christ, but the times when we can express that belonging are few and far between, because generally our vision of what wholeness means cannot embrace what is obviously flawed, the things that do not fit our usual categories of normality. Our vision of wholeness identifies it with 'perfection' — we imagine a state in which all loss and brokenness, all sin and pain and failure is wafted away, and that we think is perfection.

So we explored the idea of perfection in the work of Origen, the first Christian intellectual, a man of the Third Century. Origen believed that God must always have had his creation with him, from eternity, because if he is creator he must always have been creator. So there never was a time before God created. His creatures were in a state of perfection, spiritual beings eternally enjoying God, in perfect harmony, perfect contemplation. But it is a fact of experience that too much of a good thing means you get tired of it. The creatures became satiated, fed up, bored, and so turned their attention from God and fell. The world was created as a kind of reformatory to restore everything to a state of perfection. But there was a basic instability in Origen's system: why should the creatures not fall again? Static perfection is no use as an ideal, because the only possibility of change is loss, fall.

The terms we use like 'disability', falling short of an ideal, suggest that we know what wholeness is, but it is a similar 'static' notion. Ecumenical politics aims at the restoration of a notional state of unity or perfection, but it has never actually existed in human history, and implies the same static view. We like the 'body'-image in I Corinthians 12 because it allows diversity within the unity, but the way we read it still assumes a static perfection — like the healing of the physical body, so the healing of the ecclesiastical body, disability or division is removed and there is wholeness.

But Origen's view of cosmic wholeness was inherently unstable. It was a century or so later that one deeply influenced by Origen's theology saw what the problem was and came up with another vision — it was Gregory of Nyssa, often spoken of as a mystic. He saw that because God is infinite, you can never plumb the depths of the divine being, you can never fully know him, and so you cannot get fed up — there is always more excitement over the horizon, more to learn of him, more to enjoy. The spiritual journey is like a mountain-climb, there is always another ridge to ascend, a never-ending expedition.

This image appeals to me because of my mountaineering past, but I also recognise the draw-back: it can be a depressing thought, never to get there! But it is not like that, because each crest is a kind of perfection, a kind of wholeness, and the next target is only presented when you are in danger of falling back. This concept of perfection is dynamic, relational, has an inbuilt reciprocity involving receiving and achieving, and it is communal because there is a diversity of routes, a richness of different perspectives, and endless potential for creativity. The proper analogy for wholeness is not individual: it is the lover and beloved, of endless discovery and rediscovery of joy in one another. The Song of Songs may not appear in our modern lectionary — we are uncomfortable with an erotic love-poem in church! But for people like Origen and Gregory that poem expressed the love-songs of Christ and his bride the Church, the love-songs of God and the soul he woos.

If we take that as a parable we may be tempted to dwell on the fact that lovers fall in love and get tired of their marriage-partners — familiarity breeds contempt. And indeed if one goes into it for selfish personal fulfilment, one will probably never get full satisfaction, for a possessive love becomes deeply damaging. But a couple that retains respect for one another and enjoyment of one another find a developing delight, a constant renewal of wonder and joy, a sense of the mystery of the other, an on-going and ever-changing celebration. Even more, a couple engaged together in a common enterprise, on a journey together, a never-ending exploration, discover that wholeness is not static — it is a dynamic ever-changing thing. And it is never a self-contained perfection, because renewal happens through relationships, through mutual enjoyment of things and people outside themselves, through community. The richness of love overflows and becomes a resource that does not run out, but constantly produces the springtime of the Song of Songs.

A wholeness like that is source of growth, and it is a long way from a static or individual perfection. Besides it is a wholeness that can absorb and transfigure loss, brokenness, disability, failure, sin, hurt, death — all things that are part of the life we have been given to live. We become whole when we can live with the cross at the centre of the community. Like Paul we can then boast of our weaknesses because they show that the transforming power belongs to God, and like Paul we know that our wholeness consists in being members of one another.

Arthur has taught me this, or helped me to teach it to others. He is in a sense an instrument. But it is not just that. He belongs to the wholeness of us all, a wholeness that can embrace and absorb even deterioration and loss, because it is grounded in the infinite love of God.

The sense of call

What about the 'call' at the Dudley Road traffic-lights? Throughout Christian history there have been stories of individuals with a vocation, sometimes a vocation to stand out against the community, to challenge complacency, and disturb a static 'perfection'. Often the personal stories are modelled on Biblical precedents. And I, even I, was tempted to describe my experience in terms of the Damascus Road. I wrote a Psalm of testimony suggesting providential leading. As I engaged professionally in a study of 2 Corinthians with my colleague David Ford (the results of which were published as *Meaning and Truth in 2 Corinthians*), I found the resonances with Paul, and with the prophet Jeremiah who clearly influenced him profoundly, were greater than I had before imagined. Both Paul and Jeremiah sensed that they had been set apart before being born: I was disturbed to be told that my mother, distressed in pregnancy by the outbreak of war, had dedicated her child as Hannah did. It sharpened the mystery of 'destiny' already sensed as I found myself fulfilling the vocation of my brother Richard (see above p. 85).

At the Centre for Black and White Christian Partnership I have often heard pastors say that their ministry is not a 'profession' but a 'calling', and one by the name of Isaiah claimed to have shared the vision of his namesake. Year by year in Methodism we listen to the testimony of people who feel called to the ministry: some tell stories of that traditional 'biblical' kind, dramatic moments of realisation, and others tell of a process of 'prodding', of realising that this is what God intends them to do. The tendency of them all is to attribute specific intention and guidance to God, if not direct intervention. The stories sharpen the issue of the relationship between divine causation and human motivation.

The dark side of discipleship includes the temptation to take too much account of ourselves, to imagine that God has so directed our lives that we cease to take responsibility, or begin to 'boast' of our 'call', regarding ourselves as extra special:

> Lord, bestow on me two gifts,
>   — to forget myself,
>   — never to forget thee.
>
> Keep me from self-love, self-pity, self-will,
>   in every guise and disguise,
>   nor ever let me measure myself by myself.
>
> Save me from Self,
>   my tempter, seducer, jailer;
>   corrupting desire at the spring,
>   closing the avenues of grace,
>   leading me down the streets of death. . . .
>   (Eric Milner-White, *My God my Glory*)

Yes. History and mental hospitals are too full of megalomaniacs who believe they have a special destiny for comfort. When I ask why I was saved in a mountaineering accident when two others were killed, I hit against the mystery of coincidence: of an 'earthly' coincidence — a crevasse was conveniently placed for me to slip into when all the others tobogganed straight over it, and there was just the right delay in my flight to allow it to happen, probably caused by the person on the end of the rope engaging unsuccessfully, like the rest of us, in 'self-arrest', but checking me as a by-product; and also a 'heavenly' coincidence — for on the other side of the world, just about that time, my mother felt an urgent desire to pray for us. To leap to conclusions is to raise profound questions: what about the others? And if God 'intervenes' in one area of one's life, why not others? What about Arthur? If some 'providence' led me to 'minis-try', why did that same providence not 'save' Richard, and Arthur, and our fellow-climbers? What kind of a God is this?

Perhaps the most fascinating aspect of such things is that whereas the past can seem clear, though frighteningly mysterious, the future rarely does. The experience of trying to work out what obedience to one's vocation means, is another dark side to discipleship. And if the Bible some-times suggests divine directives, at other times we catch a glimpse of heroes of the faith struggling with what they have to do, without clear sight, often with anguish. The model of faith is setting out into the unknown like Abraham, and not arriving in the Promised Land like Moses. The climax of the list of 'faith-heroes' in Hebrews 11 is Jesus, the pioneer and perfecter of our faith, who was made like his brethren in every respect, who was tempted and tried in all points as we are, and learned through what he suffered. And there are those like Elijah who tried to run away. Isaiah speaks of a time to come yet not as yet here when 'your Teacher will not hide himself any more, but your eyes shall see your Teacher. And your ears shall hear a word behind you, saying, "This is the way, walk in it," when you turn to the right or when you turn to the left.'

One of the problems of theology has always been its desire to create system and explanation. And the balance between divine causation and human motivation, between faith and works, between destiny and responsibility, is one that has often suffered from that impetus. Making simple deductions from stories and turning them into dogmas is all too easy. The struggle between Augustine and Pelagius, Calvinism and Arminianism, even between fundamentalist and liberal, lies along this particular axis. Where we used to exercise our theological minds with the 'scandal of particularity', we now wrestle with the whole idea of divine intervention, and this issue is probably the most divisive one around in the Church today. It affects everything in the life of faith, but especially prayer of petition and intercession. The 'interveners' see God's hand everywhere, and trust him to provide a parking place when necessary; they cannot recognise that people who do not share this view have faith at all. The 'rationalisers' find difficulty in imagining any such crude involvement on God's part, and see responsibility resting with us, though effective only insofar as we are in communication with God's will for justice, peace and love.

Increasingly I find myself uneasy with either 'neat' solution. And I am intrigued by two things which may throw some oblique light on the problem. One is what they call 'chaos' research, the discovery that very little in nature follows precise and traceable patterns of cause and effect. Computer simulations of weather patterns have shown that when all the relevant conditions are known and taken account of, there may still be several different results: so weather forecasting is inherently unpredictable, and an account of cause and effect is only possible by hindsight. The sheer complexity of things allows for diversity, and the world, indeed our own body metabolism, is far from mechanical and explicable. Cancer may be the dark side of a positive 'plasticity' built into our system, and perfectly regular heartbeats are warnings of the approach of a heart attack. A certain amount of 'disaster' is necessary: stable conditions produce homogeneous species, unstable conditions produce none, but a situation which is basically stable yet may suffer disruption, as a boulder large enough to be moved by the ocean waves only under the most violent conditions, provides an environment for species variegation.

So the garden 'run wild' is a parable of a universe with possibilities; the garden neatly ordered is a parable of our desire to reduce it to categories we can grasp. We have to live without total explanation, and how much truer that must be when we are endeavouring to grasp the mystery of God and his relationship with the world. Sometimes by hindsight we may discern patterns, both on the larger scale of movements of history and on the smaller scale of personal 'direction'. But we dare not predict in detail, or think we can entirely explain. The past may give confidence for the future, but it will also question faith and hope. The only possible stance is to admit the possibility of having to walk through the valley of the shadow of death, to live by faith not sight.

And the other possible illuminator lies in our experience of human culture. The drive of much historical critical work since the Enlightenment has been to distinguish fact and interpretation, fact and myth or legend. But there are no discrete 'facts' in the end. All events and experiences are assimilated, articulated and communicated, indeed passed down to later generations, through a process of selection, of categorising according to 'stories' in the culture, of assimilation to what can be understood, explained or described by the language available.

Of course the drive to eliminate 'myth' in the sense of fantasy or illusion is important, and the analogy with the detective is illuminating. A child's description of a road accident can be compared with an adult's, and where the adult may have built in assumptions about causation, the child's lack of predetermined ideas may provide evidence which calls that into question; or the child's account may simply highlight disconnected and useless impressions which were all the child could make of the experience, whereas the adult may provide a clear picture simply because knowledge made interpretation immediate and clear. The detective may be able to reconstruct a more accurate picture of the facts by assembling many different stories from different witnesses with different levels of competence, but what he creates is still another story, and to arrive at that other story he may well have to use 'hypothesis' and 'analogy'. The 'event' or 'experience' is never discrete from 'myth' in the sense of those models of perception and explanation into which it is inexorably drawn by the human mind.

So exploring the mystery of divine involvement in our history and our lives may require many different 'stories' and the recognition that 'causation' is complex. The very way we experience things is affected by the abstraction of one 'moment' from all other insignificant moments, and the interpretation of those moments by 'models' or 'types' available to us. There is a curious interpenetration of the language and stories we have learned and the things we see and respond to, the decisions we take. The guidance of God is incarnated in the 'word' without which our experience would be meaningless. Our experience is deeply ambiguous. It has a maze-like quality, with dead-ends and unanswerable questions. Sometimes we seem to be given tenuous threads to follow through the dark, but not always. We have to penetrate the dark side of love, and the dark side of hope and the dark side of discipleship, and live through the dark night of the soul apparently alone.

The experience of ordination was an initiation into the

dark side of discipleship, a kind of prophecy of the ensuing struggle to find the way of faithfulness and obedience to the call.

The 'story' in Part A was originally told when ordination was anticipated as a profound fulfilment, and the fullness of grace was experienced at the ordination retreat:

On 2 Corinthians 3.18

The water lily flower is closed up tight.
It is a dark and cloudy day today.
The big flat leaves are floating, splashed with spray,
Undulating, trembling at their plight,
Stuck in a watery world disturbed by storms.
But yet a little while, sunshine resumes.
Responding to its warmth and light, the blooms
Uncurl and reassert their lovely forms,
Reflecting as a mirror the golden light,
Being conformed to the image of the sun
Unveiling their inner likeness to its face.
The gesture of praise! — before my sight
The petalled palms are opened; I too come
With hands uplifted, grateful for God's grace.

But between the retreat and the event I had to return to the University, rush around in the post-exam., end-of-term frenzy, face failure when I heard of a student's suicide attempt. I arrived exhausted and distraught. I could barely enter the Church, and wanted to run away. I was held to it by the gathered community, people from many different stages of my life, expectant. . . .

In the Methodist tradition ordination is symbolised by the laying on of many representative hands. I had been warned they would feel heavy. But the weight seemed to be pressing me down into a vast deep I could not understand. All I could do was cry out in my heart, 'Lord, have mercy'.

It was the very opposite of fulfilment, a quite devastating experience. It took a lot of adjusting to — even though I knew that reluctance to assume the priesthood is an old tradition: many of the Church Fathers tried to escape and had hands laid on them forcibly. It is not something to be lightly sought, and it was good for me to know that in the depths of my being.

On Psalm 102.6-7

The screech-owl hoots. Deserted ruins hear
And mocking echo its profound complaint.
Eerie the darkened world, an evil taint
Surrounds the corpse of worship. Haunting fear,
Alienation, despair compose such cries
In the waste-places of suffering, sin and death.
The wilderness spreads, breathing its hot breath
Down city streets, sounding answering sighs.
Distracted a lonely sparrow flutters and flits
From rooftop to rooftop, quite unable to rest.
There is no peace — just the deep cry of a soul
Smitten and scorched like grass, or the empty twits
Of escapism, endlessly seeking and missing the best,
Until it faces the one who hurts to make whole.

There is a darkness in the decisions forced upon us by vocation. The first was the challenge of an invitation to South Africa, the agony of choice: what was the way of righteousness? To go or not to go? To try and speak prophetically? Or to act with solidarity and observe the academic boycott? It hurt to receive a letter telling me my refusal was as though Christ had refused to come into the world because it was so sinful. One who had suffered much for South Africa told me I was not Christ, thank God! But I knew if I had been South African, I would have been enjoying the privileges of white liberal academics, and I

230

would be the same as those on whom I had passed judgment. I could only cry out in my heart, 'Lord, have mercy!'

There is a darkness through which the way has to be found: I had a vision of building theological bridges between the academic world and the world of the Church, a vision I had begun to live in the previous two years. But that summer my health went — a strange undiagnosed virus, and I had to come to terms with my handicap, the fact that I am only human, the fact that I could not do two or three jobs at once, that if I were a minister it had to be primarily as a theologian in the University. But it was the worshipping congregation which 'fed' me. I was sure that preaching was the proper mode of theological discourse. I needed to feed the flock at the communion table. The churches I was set to serve needed help. Where were the priorities?

Then there was the challenge to apply for the Professorship. Some urged me to apply, others warned against. I thought I really deeply wanted to give up as soon as possible and go to be a 'real' minister. All the pressures I had been subjected to during the process of candidating, pressures to say I would at some stage serve in Circuit (or parish work), had by now been internalised. But then someone said something that made me realise my own competitive ambition, a knot of the real me I did not like and hated to acknowledge. I shared my agony with a colleague. He looked me straight in the eye and said, 'Confess and apply'.

The personal journey to outward success and advancement has had its costly side, and still does have as I struggle with the frustrations of serving the wheels of an institution which sometimes seem as inexorable as fate itself. What does it mean to be obedient to this mysterious sense of destiny? What does it mean to identify with the poor and the oppressed? The maze is dark and sometimes we tread down dead-ends, until we see that daily attention to immediate duties and demands is the way of the servant, and that facilitating others is more important than finding our own fulfilment. The voice comes from behind saying, 'This is the way'. And the passion for theology which once seemed the way of vocation has to give way to efficient administration, and the pastoral self discovered through Arthur and through ministry in the church has to become the committee member. Passing on the baton is more important than anything else.

The problem of 'role' is one faced by many ministers in our society today. People feel 'called' to one kind of activity and find themselves thrust into another by the institutional pressures, by the traditional models and functions, by the projections and expectations of other people. Some try to be 'Jack-of-all-trades'. Some see themselves as those in society who are 'licensed to speak about God'. Some become impassioned about causes, peace, justice, liberation. Some take on the role of community worker or social worker, and sometimes it becomes difficult to distinguish the minister from those whose motivations and employment are secular. Others try to empower their lay congregations, seeing themselves as facilitators, as the hub round which the life of the local church revolves, rather than the front-line soldier. Many feel confused by the marginalisation of the churches in the life of society. Most look for some kind of 'success' and want the right 'formula' to produce results which are effective. Not a few are disillusioned by the institution they serve with its compromises and structures of tradition. Most are as worried about priorities and being sucked into mere administration as ever I have been. . . .

Two things seem to be of fundamental importance: one is recognition of the theological role of the minister — the one 'called' by God to be God's spokesperson, to 'mediate' God, tell the stories of God, help people to discern the reality of God; the other is acceptance of the vulnerability of the minister, and the need for the minister to 'receive' from those in his/her 'charge'. The first demands a new sense of the coherence of spirituality and theology, an awareness that Christian spirituality and Christian theology are expressed through Word and Sacrament, that a balance between mystery, ecstasy, and symbol on the one hand, and on the other, articulation, rationality and expression feeds heart and mind and makes the will of the person whole. No amount of 'good works' or 'social outreach' or even charismatic experience can make up for poverty at the 'centre': for 'man shall not live by bread alone, but by every word that proceeds from the mouth of God'. (These thoughts are more fully explored in *Focus on God*, co-authored with Kenneth Wilson). The second demands the humility that discerns the priesthood of Christ within the community of all believers, and allows the minister to receive absolution, love, support from those he/she serves. It means being able to discern the body and not give way to the pride and anxiety of 'going it alone'.

How these roles are to be played out in everyday decisions is bound to depend on the gifts and graces of each 'special' individual called to ministry, and the variety of situations in which such persons find themselves. There is no God-given blue-print. The maze is intricate and the passage dark, and only afterwards can we look back and discern the progress made, the keys assembled along the way. Divine initiative and human motivation twist into complex threads which offer a little tenuous guidance. But the challenge is to accept the life-lines offered by those who seem poor and handicapped and marginalised:

> I am too little, Lord,
>   to look down on others.

Chapter 12

BEYOND PASSION — THE DARK SIDE OF GOD

In these essays we have discovered the need to hold two sides of an issue together in tension over and over again: the love and wrath of God, the 'now' and the 'not yet', divine initiative and human responsibility. . . . It seems to me characteristic of Christian theology to have room for a sense of complexity and mystery, even of apparent paradox, because of such inherent tensions. Sadly through controversy there has often been a swing to dogmatic espousal of one or the other, but in the end it never satisfies. Somehow we have to live with the fact that Christ is human and divine, that the scriptures are the product of human history and culture yet the Word of God, that Christ is the fulfilment of God's promises and yet there is still sorrow and sighing, and we could multiply the examples. The theme of this chapter is that the same tension must exist in our concept of God's being: God is personal yet beyond the personal, passionate yet beyond passion. This perception has been anticipated earlier in our discomfort at the end of chapter 7 with attributing to him very human passions and reactions, and our tentative exploration in the last chapter of infinity and perfection. What follows draws on some previously published material, including an article for the Methodist Recorder.

It is not uncommon to hear sermons on the subject of God's changelessness, of a permanence behind the changes and chances of this life that is utterly dependable. It is a fundamentally biblical idea, expressing God's faithfulness and his unchanging love. It is an important devotional concept, and traditionally it has been an important theological concept. Whereas this world is trapped in change, in Becoming, God is totally other — he is Being, beyond change, eternal and perfect. Nowadays, however, this 'static' view of God is increasingly challenged. The 'process theologians' have spoken of a God who develops in response to his creation; liberation theologians have spoken of a God who suffers alongside the poor (the changeless God, it is said, prevents change in society); and theologians like Moltmann have spoken of 'The Crucified God', of a God revealed in Christ in such a way that pain and suffering must in some sense be attributed to the divine being itself.

So what is regarded as the old 'philosophical' concept of God as perfect, therefore unchangeable, therefore impassible, has come under fire from a number of angles, many of which one feels one must approve. Is it not true that the God of the Old Testament is affected by the disobedience of his people and yearns for them in love? How could a personal God not be involved, and therefore truly suffer in response to the sufferings of his creatures? Above all, isn't the Cross the supreme revelation of the nature of the God we worship?

Such reflections are reinforced for many by experience. For one reason or another, people are brought to the point of asking the question, 'Why, O why? If there is a God of love who created this world, why is there so much suffering?' And when the hurt goes deep, all the traditional slick answers seem useless: 'It's a way of testing and proving us: suffering brings greater maturity; it has a positive role.' That has some point, though it feels sometimes a bit sadistic on God's part, and it breaks down when you see how often it has the opposite negative effect: a greater proportion of marriages break up when the family has to cope with a handicapped child — the one tragedy produces another and becomes the harder to cope with. Nor does it help to attribute the 'gonewrongness' either to the devil or the effects of human sin: for some disasters human beings are clearly not responsible — they are part of the nature of the universe, and if God be God, he must be responsible for creating that situation; and indeed, if there be a devil, he must be responsible for the devil's existence. So for many sufferers, the only answer is the Cross — the fact of God suffering, God entering into all the travail and pain, taking responsibility for it, overcoming it. The suffering God is not just a theological theory, but a devotional necessity.

So away with the God of the philosophers, goes up the cry: What has Athens to do with Jerusalem? What has Plato to do with the God of the Bible? It is not the first time such sentiments have been expressed in Christian theology: those were virtually the words of Tertullian, the first Christian to write in Latin rather than Greek. But nevertheless, Tertullian took it for granted that ultimately God was impassible, and was deeply offended by the Modalists who identified, as modes of one God, the Father, the Son and the Spirit: 'they crucify the Father and put the Paraclete to flight', he mocked. It is worth enquiring why this other view has been so persistent. As one who has written about God's suffering, I have to confess that there remains a niggling worry that God's changelessness and impassibility remain important ideas. For how can a vulnerable God still be God, a God to worship and depend upon? If you are tempted to sigh 'Poor old God', what kind of a God are you left with?

The difficult questions posed by the idea of God suffering are well explored by Paul S. Fiddes in *The Creative Suffering of God* (OUP 1988). To struggle with these ideas at a deep level is important if we are not to be merely sentimental about God's suffering. In the end Fiddes follows the general trend of modern theology in attributing suffering to God. One of the most important arguments for challenging the traditional view of God's changelessness is that our experience of relationships between people, of people affecting one another, sympathising with one another, and so on, always involves change. So if God is love, he must be involved: he must therefore be subject to change. The pictures of God as an uninvolved 'do-gooder' will not do.

But even if we stick to human analogies, perhaps we have to work with a more complex picture. We are ambivalent in our evaluation of our own emotions. On the one hand we regard feelings as giving 'depth' to our experience, and we value joy and loving concern, even pain when it softens and humanises: we don't admire insensitivity. But on the other hand, we distrust stormy emotions and one of our ideals is peace, peace of mind and serenity, the ability to ride the storms of passion which are so often fuelled by self-will or self-concern. We live with this tension in our self-perception quite happily, and a musical analogy may help us to grasp how. Music seems naturally to express emotion: the keening lament of the mourner, or the dance of celebration, or the emotional longing of romantic music. But in reaction modern musicians have been exploring pure sound, and the true 'classics' like Bach or Mozart, might be said to explore pure form. Strangely enough, though they are not romantics and should not be played romantically, that very search for 'order' — almost mathematical precision — is full of 'feeling': so peace is not inanimate but full of joy, and we can imagine a 'passionless passion'.

And strangely enough this can be most profoundly true in pastoral relationships: it is not for nothing that 'non-involvement' has been preached as a virtue. Early in 1988, a couple close to me had a tragic experience in relation to the birth of a child — their daughter was still-born. To say the least I felt for them. But after a while I realised that my distress was not just for them. I was re-living my own pain, my own struggle to understand how things could go wrong, my own anguish and protest at the suffering of the world. I was too involved, and it was only when the self-involvement was purged that I could begin to be of use to those who were suffering.

From that experience I found myself reclaiming the insight that God is 'beyond suffering' in the sense that he is not emotionally involved in a self-concerned way — rather he is that ocean of love that can absorb all the suffering of the world and purge it without being polluted or changed by it. And yet at the same time in Christ he subjected himself to personal involvement in pain and anguish, so that in some sense he genuinely knows what it feels like to be victim and shares in our experience of suffering. The two ideas somehow belong together, and (despite the conclusions of Fiddes) our knowledge of God is impoverished if we cannot stretch our minds and imaginations to encompass both.

SEA PIECES

I

The sound of the sea is an endless fascination
A kind of tense repose that disturbs imagination
Deep calling to deep in constant expectation.

The sound of the sea stimulates relaxation
A kind of restless space for active contemplation
Deep calling to deep in visible meditation.

The sound of the sea encourages celebration
A kind of eternal time in rhythmic concentration
Wave surmounting wave in harmonic intonation
Deep calling to deep in symphonic jubilation

II

Around the cliffs the caves of seabird settlements
The screams of circling gulls
Echo and reverberate
    echo and reverberate
As the screams of children playing
    screams of fear and laughter
And screams of families fraying
    screams of love and anger
Echo and reverberate
    echo and reverberate
Around the walls and ways of human tenements.

But after the storm and the wild overnight gales
Around the cliffs and caves of seabird settlements
There echoes and reverberates
    booms and resonates
The thunder of roaring breakers
Drowning the screams of gulls
As the thunder of warring conflict
Echoes and reverberates
    booms and resonates
Drowning the screams of children playing
Drowning the screams of families fraying
In a mightier roar of pain
That echoes and reverberates
    booms and resonates
Around the walls and ways of human tenements.

Around the cliffs and caves of seabird settlements
The infinite swell of the ocean
Absorbs and assimilates
    absorbs and assimilates
The screams of circling gulls
As ripples on the surface of the waves.
So the infinite swell of God's love
Absorbs and assimilates
    resolves and sublimates
The screams of joy and anger

  screams of pain and hunger
The screams of fear and need
  screams of fun and greed
Screams of excitement
  and screams of indictment
Screams of deprivation
  and screams of elation
The infinite swell of God's love
Absorbs and assimilates
  resolves and sublimates
As ripples on the waves of eternity
Around the walls and ways of human tenements.

III

The sea, a destructive creating power,
Carves out coastlines hour by hour,
Restless its constant activity.
The sea, a boundless rising swell,
Captures minds and casts its spell,
Deep its untold mystery.

Booming in chasms and hollow caves,
Throwing up its sparkling spray,
Catching the sunlight it glistens and gleams,
Reflecting the clouds it seems gloomy and grey;
Ebbing and flowing its boiling tide,
Cascading foam over each rock,
Rolling white breakers to the shore,
Sustaining life where seabirds flock;
Roaring a salty haze in the air,
Churning stones in its surge and suck,
Tossing seaweed in its surf,
It plays with floats that bob and duck.

Tempting kids to romp in its waves,
Daring people to swim and play;
Coaxing men to fish in teams
For abundant resources that pay their way;
Carrying man-made vessels who've plied
Their dirty trade from dock to dock

In hopes of making more and more
To stack behind a security lock
Without obligation to play it fair
Only to gamble with chance and luck;
It demands respect for all its worth
Absorbing countless gallons of muck.

IV

The sea, an immense and playful giant,
To moon and wind responsive, pliant,
Yet with profound integrity.

Is like that infinite ocean of grace
That surging tide which must give place
To be exploited and be free.

That awful creative love unknown
Holy, hidden, only shown
In ripples of still small secrecy.

That passionless deep beyond all sense
That rages with passion deep and intense,
Mercy in wrath's serenity.

V

To be by the sea is an endless fascination
A kind of restless peace that imparts exhilaration
Deep responding to deep with increasing exultation.

To be by the sea excites admiration
A kind of awful joy and ecstatic sublimation
Deep responding to deep with profound inner prostration.

To be by the sea is to join in veneration
A kind of endless praise for the wonder of creation
Wave reflecting wave in silent celebration
Deep responding to deep in endless circulation.

Why did the early thinkers of the Church insist on the impassibility of God?

To appreciate the point it is important to recall the myths of the Greeks. It certainly was not for nothing that philosophers in the ancient world criticised the colourful presentation of the gods we find there — superhuman human beings, with all their passions and desires, producing heroes by intercourse with human women, meddling in human affairs, subjecting people to their arbitrary tyrannies and exacting powers, and yet depending on their underlings for sacrifices and honours. . . . The truly divine must be different, beyond bribery and corruption, beyond deception, consistent and therefore beyond emotional reactions and not subject to being swayed or affected by beings outside the divine self. The truly divine cannot be men and women writ large:

> Ethiopians make their gods black with turned up noses. Thracians make them with red hair and blue eyes; mortals think that gods are born and have their own food, voice and shape; but if oxen or lions had hands and could draw or produce images like men, horses would draw the shapes of the gods like horses, oxen like oxen, and they would produce such bodies as the bodily frame they have themselves.

So wrote Xenophanes in the sixth century BC, and other fragments survive in which Homer and Hesiod are criticised for attributing to the gods human faults like stealing, adultery and mutual deception. We hear that Xenophanes asserted there must be one god who is quite unlike mortals in form and thought, and accounts describe this god as eternal, unoriginated (i.e. never came into being but always was), impassible (not subject to influence, pain, emotion, change, etc.), as one and everything, as neither finite or infinite, neither moved nor at rest, but the greatest and best of all things. Probably late witnesses have assimilated Xenophanes' language to developed philosophical ideas, but already such notions were clearly being anticipated, and they are associated with a radical and necessary criticism of anthropomorphism, the concept of gods in human form.

This criticism of anthropomorphism, coupled with Plato's moral objections to the traditional gods of mythology, made a significant contribution to the development of the so-called philosophical idea of God that the early Christian thinkers inherited: a monotheistic doctrine of a transcendent Being with largely negative attributes. That God has no beginning or end, is beyond time and place, has no needs and, being perfect, is unchangeable, are deliberate points of contrast to the gods of popular religion. Early Christian thinkers would have echoed their pagan contemporary Maximus of Tyre in asserting:

> He is the Mind which is Father and Maker of All, whose name Plato cannot tell because he does not know it, whose appearance he cannot describe because he cannot see it; whose size he cannot estimate, since he cannot touch it. 'The divine is invisible to the eyes, unspeakable with the voice, untouchable with the flesh, unknown to the hearing: only by the most beautiful, most pure, most intellectual . . . aspect of the soul is it seen through its likeness and heard through its kinship, the whole together being present to the whole understanding . . .' God has no size, no colour, no form, nor any other accident of matter, but he has a beauty unlike any other beauty.

Early Christian thinkers were properly persuaded that the God of the Bible could be described thus. For in the prophetic tradition of Israel there had been a parallel critique of idolatry and inadequate popular notions of God's reactions, for example, to sacrifice. To think one could live as one liked regardless of the covenant law and then bribe God with sacrificial gifts was the butt of Amos' criticism, and a century and more later, the prophet whose words are recorded in the later chapters of Isaiah produced a brilliant parody of idolatry:

244

The carpenter stretches a line, he marks it out with a pencil; he fashions it with planes, and marks it with a compass; he shapes it into the figure of a man. . . . He cuts down cedars . . . Half of it he burns in the fire . . . he roasts meat . . . also he warms himself and says, 'Aha, I am warm, I have seen the fire!' And the rest of it he makes into his god . . . and worships it . . .; he prays to it and says, 'Deliver me, for thou art my god!'

In fact, Jewish fear of blasphemy, respect for the unnameable God, and deep religious sense of a transcendent holiness and otherness went further than Greek philosophy towards recognising God's infinity and essential incomprehensibility. 'My thoughts are higher than your thoughts and my ways than your ways.' 'No-one can see God and live.' Even Moses was hidden in a cleft while God's glory passed by — he could only see his backparts. And this transcendent holy God, utterly other than his creatures, was consistent and faithful, just and incorruptible. Of course he was 'beyond passion'.

Yet the Bible speaks much of a 'man-like' God, a God who is angry and sometimes vindictive, a God with voice and hands, who walks in the garden in the cool of the evening, a God who, according to Hosea, loves and woos his harlot-bride Israel. Pagan critics of Christianity exploited all this, as did some Christians who wished to abandon the Old Testament. But it was a bit like the pot calling the kettle black. Popular religion whether pagan, Jewish or Christian, tended to be 'anthropomorphic'; philosophic religion by this time, whether pagan, Jewish or Christian, accepted popular forms of religious language as pointing to something other, using allegory and insisting that the divine being in itself could not be so conceived.

So they all exploited the Platonic view that there were three ways to knowledge of God: by synthesis, analysis and

245

analogy. Synthesis proceeded by observing the highest and most beautiful things of creation, and moving to the beauty of immaterial things like the soul, and then contemplating the vast ocean of the beautiful so as to conceive of what is truly good, lovable and desirable. Analysis used the technique of abstraction, taking away what we know, 'negativing' our earthly experience and knowledge to arrive at an awareness of that which is other (the 'apophatic' way already discussed which insists that God is invisible, incorporeal, untouchable, impassible, incorruptible, etc.). Analogy meant creating 'myths' or 'similes', such as Plato's description of the sun in the Republic, or the Demiurge in the Timeaus.

Christian theology was the more insistent that God was beyond the capacity of human knowledge, because this gave an opening for insisting that God is only known through revelation. God in himself is in principle infinite and incomprehensible: but he has chosen to 'accommodate' himself to our human level, speak to us in human language, even meet us as a human being in Jesus. The impersonal God, the impassible transcendent unknown 'Other', allowed us to relate to him as personal, became passible, offering himself to us as one vulnerable to whatever we would do to him — and was handed over to death on a cross. Perhaps we can only do justice to this mystery by regaining a sense of seriousness about the mystery of the Trinity. The theism of Western theology has proved itself powerless in the face of the atheist critique, not least because it has vainly tried to uphold the view that God is personal. That is a sophisticated form of anthropomorphism. Impersonal images, such as 'ocean' or 'rock' may at first sight seem even less satisfactory, but they are needed if we are to grasp what it means to speak of God as not limited to any of our conceptions. Eastern theology has much to teach us on this score. God cannot be known in his 'essence', say the classic Greek Fathers, but he is known through his activities. He is impassible in his 'essence', but became 'passible' in Christ, who as both human and divine, 'unsufferingly suffered', or experienced a 'passionless passion'.

The effect of this kind of thinking is interesting. There was a strong movement to 'allegorise' away the wrath and anger of God, along with his hands and feet — for anger is 'being in a passion' and 'reacting' to outside stimulus in an uncontrollable way: such could not happen to God, it was felt. On the other hand, those most anxious to remove God's anger, emphasised his 'love'. But that meant purifying human conceptions of love from all jealousy and possessiveness, from anger and upset at disappointment, seeing it as an 'outflow' rather than a 'passion'. So God's love was seen in his providential and saving activity. But that included his activity of 'discipline': for a loving Father does not let his wayward children get away with it, for their own good. The movement of 'denial' and 'affirmation' was essential, and the only proper procedure by which any religious language could function. Human analogies had to be refined by an appropriate critique. But given that critique, highly realistic anthropomorphisms were permissible. Perhaps we should not throw away the keys collected in chapter 7, but collect some more corrective keys to add to the bunch.

For good reason classical Christian theology has acknowledged the dark side of God, the mystery of his unknown Being, beyond our grasp. And mystical theology has exploited the images of entering the darkness, and of the dark night of the soul. Eastern liturgies have characterised God as good and loving towards humanity (philanthropos), as merciful, kindly and gracious, as the patron of the

247

weak and Saviour. But he is so because he is not given to favouritism, or easily deceived, or susceptible to bribes. Negative attributes balance the positive ones: he is not limited by time or origin, nor is his being, power or authority derivative — all Greek adjectives beginning with the equivalent of in- or un-. God is incomparable and unapproachable, uncircumscribed, unchangeable: his power is unequalled, his glory incomprehensible, his mercy immeasurable, his love inexpressible. The negatives enhance the sense of transcendent otherness, and so highlight the wonder of his condescension in becoming a help to the helpless, saviour of the tempest-tossed, harbour for the sailor, doctor for the sick.

When I heard within me 'It makes no difference to me whether you believe in me or not', it was a reminder of God's independence of our perception or acknowledgment of him. The reality of God is not identical with any of our 'models' of his Being. The autobiography of Thomas Merton provides a fascinating example of how such a realisation can be converting. He was a typical 'modern' young man in the interwar years, sceptical about religion (especially as he could discern in it the projection of human anxieties and desires), and full of the joys of life, ambitious, sociable, you name it. . . . But he was open-minded enough to read a little Mediaeval philosophy. There he discovered the 'aseity' of God: the fact that God is, as Latin would put it, *a se* 'of himself' — not dependent on anyone or anything, beyond the conception of anyone, that he just IS, and is himself not what we project onto him. In other words, God needs no defender. Thomas Merton could not turn his back on such a God, and it was my moment of release to grasp the same point in a radical way, and so be absolved of responsibility and released from doubt. I guess Job's answer is somewhat similar: Job couldn't let God be God, but trapped him in his questions, until confronted with his reality. The dark side of God then mysteriously becomes the light that sheds abroad his love in a dark world, and there is no hiding place.

> The darkness is no darkness with you, but the night is as clear as day. The darkness and the light are both alike.
> (Ps. 139)

The first thing the Greek Fathers thought of when worshipping God or thinking of him was his abundant and inexhaustible goodness. That is what is known through his acts and his activities, even as he remains in himself a transcendent and mysterious being. Description of this overflowing love is consistently made possible, despite divine transcendence, by blowing up the highest ideals of human love:

> God speaks of the love of birds for their young, the love of fathers for their children, the tenderness of mothers, not because he only loves like a mother loves her child, but because we have no greater proofs of love than these examples,

suggested the great preacher John Chrysostom in his Homilies on the Psalms. He shows how the image of the spiritual marriage not only enabled the Fathers to appropriate the erotic language of the Song of Songs, but also to speak of the Psalmist as lover. God is worshipped in song and celebration; it is impossible to see him — so the Psalmist composes songs, communicating with him through odes and hymns, kindling the desire of many others: lovers are always like this — singing love-songs when they cannot see the loved one. So praise results from thinking the things of God, appreciating his blessings — and yet also from a

249

certain elusiveness, indirectness, focussing not on God himself who is beyond our perception, but on the evidence of his loving activities.

So 'our chief theological knowledge is confessing that we have none' (as Cyril of Jerusalem instructed his catechumens, new Christians in training for baptism). The way through the maze is open-ended, the mountaineering expedition is never-ending — simply because God is infinite and so in principle cannot be defined, grasped or fully known. It is not the arriving that matters but the journeying, and celebrating on that journey the tantalising mystery and goodness of one who remains elusive yet has visited us in Christ, and calls and enlightens each one of us.

Lighten our darkness, we beseech thee, O Lord: and by thy great mercy defend us from all perils and dangers of this night; for the love of thy only Son, our Saviour, Jesus Christ. Amen.

For God, who commanded the light to shine out of darkness, hath shined in our hearts, to give the light of the knowledge of the glory of God in the face of Jesus Christ.

SALISBURY CATHEDRAL IN RECOLLECTION

Golden beams slanting askew:
    a step through the door
into dark cavernous space
    and suddenly coolness.

Golden cross beaming from far:
    a gasp at the light
against dark jigsaws of glass
    for prisoners of conscience.

250

Golden sun rippling below:
 a thrill at the tones
of the cloth, broidery rich,
 its radiance diffusing.

Golden crown blazing in midst:
 a pain at the thorns
in the bright brilliant heart
 of art's composition.

Golden chalice beaming with fire:
 a cry from the deep
at the cup's soul-piercing ray
 in evening's keen glory.

Golden bush burning with light:
 a presence revealed
in the dark cavernous world,
 and sudden vocation.